Endorsem
A Nobler Side of Leadership:

M000280999

"Linda Belton played a key role to help make Servant-Leadership the model for the Veterans Administration moving forward. This is a book that not only captures that journey, it also includes personal formative questions and assessments. A must read should you want to embark upon the journey to become a Servant Leader in your organization."

Joseph M. Patrnchak, Author of *The Engaged Enterprise,* Principal Green Summit Partners and former Chief Human Resource Officer, Cleveland Clinic

"Books are vehicles for innovative ideas and the launch of conversations otherwise missed. *A Nobler Side of Leadership: The Art of Humanagement,* is that vehicle and more! Linda Belton gives us the gift of her talent and skills in stories, concepts, tool box activities, and practice sets that should be required for all leaders. Linda is a role model in Servant Leadership, and we are fortunate to have a vehicle for her wisdom!"

Terri Morris-Nichols, System Director of Risk Management, Peace-Health; faculty in Servant Leadership, St. Joseph's College

"Linda Belton, a Servant Leader to her very core, has written *A Nobler Side of Leadership, The Art of Humanagement* to share her considerable experience with and insights about Servant Leadership. The book is informative and practical, but even better, there is a genuine presence to Belton's writing that makes it personal, lively, and very readable. Her book embodies the same spirit of service that she writes about; it will help every reader be a better leader."

Anthony L. Suchman, MD, MA, Senior Consultant and Founder, Relationship Centered Health Care

"Over and over Belton gives intensely useful examples of leadership. She speaks in terms of everyday experiences that persons in any field and at every level can relate to. The book is interesting and easy on the eye; the graphics are enlivening but uncomplicated. The particulars of Servant Leadership are present and strong, and woven throughout the book. Belton's style is 'real' and profoundly simple, yet answers so many plaguing questions that swirl around sound management practices. This is a book for all readers in any professional setting."

Diane Wegner, MS Educational Leadership, Fmr Dir, SSM Associates

"Linda Belton has written a compelling book about her research, practice, and reflection on the positive power of Servant Leadership. This book will be an important resource for both the novice and the long time practitioner. Servant Leadership is timely and timeless and this book captures both. Linda's commitment to make every day Veteran's day is an example of how meaningful, ethical, and practical servant leadership is in our personal, professional, and institutional lives. This work challenges and affirms the developing Servant Leadership movement."

Thomas A. Thibodeau, Distinguished Professor of Servant Leadership, Viterbo University

"*A Nobler Side of Leadership: The Art of Humanagement* provides a pragmatic approach to implementing Servant Leadership in an organization. Having worked with Ms. Belton, I know firsthand that she lives and breathes these principles. Ms. Belton has presented a compelling model for demonstrating that there is connectivity in everything we do. This is an excellent model to make your organization a place where employees thrive and patients and their families are welcome."

Nevin M. Weaver, Healthcare Consultant and Executive Coach

"Linda Belton's book describes the "soft" skills of management, which often presents a hard challenge for leaders. While cogently explaining the theoretical constructs behind her thinking, her book is packed with specific examples, clear instructions, and pragmatic suggestions for improving your managerial style. Linda Belton is truly one of the very best Servant Leaders you will ever meet!"

Dee Ramsel, PhD, MBA, Director VHA National Center for Organization Development

"Linda Belton eloquently shares her expertise in all things Servant Leadership in this thought-provoking, practice - reflective and change agent publication. Real time application to every day challenges in the ever-evolving work environment is provided for all, regardless of one's position in an organization. Personal insights from her life experiences in developing what she coins "humanagement" can be easily applied as well to the readers' personal lives, strengthening family and community relationships. Foundational strategies in living well, growing healthy organizations and productive societies can all be gleaned from this inspirational work. I recommend the inclusion of *A Nobler Side of Leadership: The Art of Humanagement* in any organization's leadership education curriculum and for employees at all levels."

Cynthia L. Murray BN RN-BC, American Academy of Ambulatory Care Nurses (AAACN) Leadership Board Member, Veterans Health Administration Ambulatory Care Nursing

"It feels like a very personal swim through what is for many a large, murky, and often confusing sea. It's especially useful as an introduction for someone who is not happy with their own management practice, but unsure where to begin. *A Nobler Side of Leadership: The Art of Humanagement* provides a road map to a large body of literature and techniques that help the reader grow into success."

Michael J. Hodgson, MD, Chief Consultant for Occupational Health

"Linda Belton has done an outstanding job of explaining Servant Leadership and its tremendous value in the workplace, including actionable information the reader can easily implement. Grounded in Linda's years of impressive experience researching and advancing Servant Leadership within the Department of Veterans Affairs, *A Nobler Side of Leadership* is both a thorough explanation of this transformative approach to leading and a practical guide for developing it within your own organization. She clearly explains today's need for a fundamental re-imagining of corporate culture and organizational health, presenting a compelling case for Servant Leadership as a core component of tomorrow's successful, values-based organizations. We highly recommend this book for business leaders, leadership consultants, and trainers."

Jenny Young, Conductor, Harmony Crew Consultants, LLC

"Linda Belton shares hard-won insights that can help anyone to introduce servant leadership into their organizations. She presents a valuable case study, including specific tools that she and her colleagues developed to promote a servant leadership culture in a large, complex organization. The book describes how wisdom and compassion can be applied to practical problems and move an organization to higher levels of service."

Dr. Kent M. Keith, President Emeritus, Greenleaf Center for Servant Leadership and author, *The Case for Servant Leadership*

"Buy this book! *A Nobler Side of Leadership: The Art of Humanagement* is the new handbook for implementing servant leadership in organizations, written by a seasoned practitioner. Moreover, it is a great read. With deep wisdom and good cheer, Linda Belton uses stories, diagrams, art, reflections, organizational and servant leadership principles, checklists, toolbox activities, and more stories to explain how she and her team established a foundation for servant leadership at Veterans Administration hospitals. She does not ignore the well-publicized problems in VA hospitals but draws lessons from them. Lessons you can use. Along the way you will learn a prescription for healthy organizations where everyone can be a leader, how "all things are connected," why accountability is what Dr. Ann McGee-Cooper called "the taproot of servant leadership," how to answer objections to servant leadership as you patiently lead the way, and how "*Servant Leadership is not about a single style of leading: it is a philosophy and a practice that overarches all styles of leading.* It colors how we hire and fire, plan and hold accountable, think and behave, relate and communicate." Mostly, though, you will be inspired to read the book again and immediately use what you have learned."

Don M. Frick, PhD; Author, *Implementing Servant Leadership: Stories from the Field*, co-author, *Seven Pillars of Servant Leadership: Practicing the Wisdom of Leading by Serving*

A Nobler Side of Leadership: The Art of Humanagement

A Servant Leader Journey

A Nobler Side of Leadership: The Art of Humanagement
A Servant Leader Journey

Copyright © Linda Belton 2016
All rights reserved.

ISBN 13: 978-1-944338-02-2

Book design by Adam Robinson and Adrienne Belton

Published by The Greenleaf Center for Servant Leadership
133 Peachtree St. NE, Suite 350
Atlanta, GA 30303
www.greenleaf.org

Dedicated to Alex
Who makes all things possible.

Thanks to Adrienne for her immaculate editing,
artistic design and loving encouragement.

Thanks to Marc for his overview and analysis,
wise counsel and unfailing confidence.

They are the very best part of me.

A companion Workbook with additional interactive tools, activities, and resources is available for purchase.

Designed to accompany the book, the Workbook adapts the content to a learner-friendly format, where individuals and groups, on their own or with facilitation, can experience it at a more personal level.

For information about the Workbook or additional materials, please contact belton.leadership@gmail.com.

CONTENTS

A NOBLER SIDE OF LEADERSHIP:
THE ART OF HUMANAGEMENT

A Servant Leader Journey

Linda W. Belton

ROBERT K. GREENLEAF
CENTER FOR
SERVANT LEADERSHIP

INTRODUCTION

The terms of the work world have changed. Employee expectations and organizational mandates have shifted. In order to be successful and relevant in this environment, leaders must learn new ways of leading, throwing off the old command and control styles of management and adopting models that are principled, progressive and service-driven. That requires more than a to-do list: it demands a fundamental re-imagining of corporate culture and Organizational Health. Drawing upon the Greenleaf model of Servant Leadership, *A Nobler Side of Leadership: The Art of Humanagement* offers a fresh approach to meeting the critical leadership challenges of contemporary organizations, while honoring the humanity of everyone they touch.

Servant Leadership is not a new idea, but it is being "discovered" at an exponential rate. Contemporary organizations are eagerly searching for guidance in achieving their missions and goals through engaged and invested employees; employees who become co-creators of the organization. To meet those challenges, companies cannot rely solely on a small cadre of managers at the top: it requires *every* person to be a leader in his/her own right. In today's world, no one gets a pass.

A Nobler Side of Leadership: The Art of Humanagement studies the massive, highly scrutinized Department of Veterans Affairs (VA) on its Servant Leader journey. This is not a portrait of an organization that has "made it" to Servant Leader status, but one that is a "work-in-progress." It represents the struggles with which most companies—private and public alike—can identify.

The text relies on real-life situations and illuminating stories of success as well as failure, from both personal and organizational perspectives, candidly detailing hard-won insights. While examples are taken from health care and government, "Reality Checks ✓" peppered throughout the narrative help readers translate the learning to their own environment. The book combines high-level principles with practical tips, All Things Connected "op-ed" pieces, toolbox activities and interactive materials for individuals and small groups. Significant, replicable products and instruments are provided for the reader's use, including the entire content of VA's unique 360 Degree Assessment.

In the earlier chapters, themes of Organizational Health and Servant Leadership are broadly explored. Chapter Six introduces the new concept of *Humanagement,* a novel approach to pairing the hard skills of management with the essential leadership function of building relationships, and develops the theme further in related sections on *Humenvironment* and *Humanopoly.* Later chapters are devoted to the spiritual dimension of Servant Leadership, an aspect seldom acknowledged in leadership literature, and often a taboo subject in the workplace, and to the attainment of a society in which *we're all leaders, all the time.*

A Nobler Side of Leadership: The Art of Humanagement helps traditional/positional leaders to understand their obligations as stewards and servants, yet expands that audience to anyone with a desire to serve, regardless of hierarchical status. It will be of interest to C-Suite executives and other leaders with enterprise-wide impact who seek to transform the workplace. Mid-and lower-level managers and supervisors will use the book to create cohesive teams, improve the work environment and to develop themselves for roles of greater responsibility. Importantly, it will also be of value to employees or organization members who are committed to "leading in place": demonstrating the principles of Servant Leadership and a personal investment in being part of the change they want to see, wherever they happen to be. Enlightened leaders at any level, and those who are pursuing enlightenment, will be drawn to the premises of this book as a better way of doing business.

Organizational change begins with individuals. Individuals who understand and practice the nobler side of leadership can change their workplaces and communities. The impact comes through consistent modeling and messaging of the behaviors that make us *finer*.

A Nobler Side of Leadership: The Art of Humanagement aims to recognize the connections between power, relationships, mission and the bottom line; to help workplaces become Servant Organizations. It hopes to inspire greater job satisfaction and engagement among employees, a consciously humane business climate, and the development of potential Servant Leaders to guide our future.

—Linda W. Belton

CHAPTER ONE

A Journey—Not a Race

A Health Care Parable on "Do Unto Others"...

The Ruler of the Realm had been plagued for months with intractable back pain and reluctantly decided to travel the day's journey to the Medical Center for help.

After a grueling trek, he parked his carriage (with difficulty) and presented himself to the Admissions window.

He was not recognized for who he was, and was directed to have a seat in the waiting room until the clinic staff had time to see him.

It was a busy day and people were working hard, but after an hour his back could not endure the wait and he approached the desk to find out how long it would be.

Frustrated, the clerk called a nurse, remarking in a whispered (but overheard) aside that this was a problem patient and would the nurse please take him off the clerk's hands?!

The Ruler was led to a treatment room where he was poked, prodded and questioned. Being naïve in the mysteries of medicine, he was somewhat anxious and not at all sure what was expected of him.

In confusion, he blurted out that his discomfort was intolerable and all he wanted was something to relieve the pain. The nurse firmly told him that drugs were not the answer, and left to consult a doctor about the patient's "drug-seeking" behavior.

An x-ray was ordered and the ride to Radiology was a nightmare. The transportation aide bumped down the corridors, seemingly unaware of the Ruler's discomfort, and bewailed the latest hospital budget cuts, not something the Ruler wanted to hear at that moment!

His spine was photographed and after a lengthy delay, the radiologist reported that the films showed hypertrophic changes to T5-T9 , with lateral scoliotic tendencies and neural entrapment; that he was not a candidate for electrical stimulation or laminectomy; that apart from exercise, nothing could be done and the Ruler would have to learn to live with the pain.

Alarmed and dazed, the Ruler beseeched the physician to explain in language he could understand, but she was already hurrying off to see the next patient.

Some leaflets and a prescription for Physical Therapy were thrust into his hand and he was reminded to stop at the Cashier's office on the way out.

While leaving, the Ruler became faint and braced himself against the wall for support.

For minutes he remained this way until a housekeeper stopped to inquire if he needed assistance. The housekeeper helped the Ruler to the cafeteria for a cup of coffee and, when he had recovered, guided him through the maze of hallways to the parking lot where his carriage was waiting.

Sadly, the Ruler returned to his palace, picking up the painful thread of his existence.

*   *   *

Every Tuesday it was the Ruler's custom to open the doors of the palace and entertain petitions from the citizens of the Realm. Today among the petitioners, he was surprised to recognize the Admissions clerk from the Medical Center. The clerk was distraught over the condition of her office, which was cramped, dark, hot and poorly equipped, causing her much discomfort. Renovation of the office had been postponed due to other construction priorities.

"You, Sir," she said, "have the power to reverse those priorities so I don't have to wait any longer."

"Waiting was not your concern when others were doing the waiting," he responded. "You raised not a finger to welcome me or ameliorate my delay. Your office will be repaired, but you will wait for it to be so." And he dismissed her from his sight.

When the second petitioner entered, the Ruler was shocked to see the clinic nurse who had labeled him as a "drug seeker." The nurse pled eloquently that budget cuts were at the root of the problem, that money was being diverted to other departments and that his clinic was not receiving its fair share. He was here to solicit an endowment. The Ruler immediately wrote off the nurse as a "complainer" and took relish in saying, "Dollars are not the answer," then sent him on his way.

Then the third petitioner presented himself: the radiologist who had no time to answer the Ruler's questions and quiet his fears. The physician was enraged about a new Policy of the Realm which was fraught with royal mumbo-jumbo, and which might have disastrous effects on her practice and remuneration. "This threatens to create major changes in my established routines and activities," she protested, "but the law is so obscure that I cannot understand what to do about it. As Ruler, you are obliged to make it clear."

The Ruler's sympathy for the physician was great, but the opportunity to confer a lesson was greater.

"Inability to comprehend and control the changes in one's own life," he mused, "is often more tormenting than the change itself. Yes, the new law demands adjustments, but I simply don't have time to discuss them." And he called the last petitioner.

The housekeeper was ushered in and bright smiles lit both their faces. The housekeeper opened his mouth to speak, but the Ruler hushed him. "Before you ask, I will tell you that whatever you desire is yours. You alone had compassion for me, though you knew me not. You left your appointed rounds to offer me an arm, some nourishment and a moment of your time. What is it you wish?"

"I have two requests," replied the housekeeper. "First, I ask that you not judge our Medical Center harshly, as many fine and caring people work there, and that you would grant the desires of the petitioners who came before me." The Ruler agreed, and he proceeded to renovate all work spaces, make whole the budget and rectify all illogical policies.

What was the second wish, you wonder? It was to be sent to school to learn the ancient art of acupuncture, whereupon he healed the Ruler's back pain and received the highest honors of the Realm.

...All Things Connected

The Long and Winding Road...
—The Beatles

This book has been 40 years in the making. It is not meant to be a scholarly work, but the story of my journey as an aspiring Servant Leader. I do not consider myself an expert—I leave that designation to those who have been Servant Leaders in my life, those who have inspired me to set out on the journey, hold fast when the terrain seemed impassable and who continue to cheer me on to the finish. The finish line is a goal, but not a realistic expectation: the challenge and the joy are clearly in the striving. Some may count retirement as the finish line, but I achieved that status recently and let me assure you I'm not done yet!

My milieu, the work environment with which I am familiar, is health care. I have not researched case studies of Servant Leadership in the corporate or non-profit world (there are many excellent books available—see Patrnchak, Sipe and Frick, Jennings and others). And I will not attempt a discourse on Greenleaf's writings beyond the basics of Servant Leadership (see Keith, Spears and others) and the tenets that have informed my own work. My aim, then, is to share, in a simple but authentic style, where I have been and what I have learned along the way. My hope is that the reader may benefit from my successes and my slip-ups, transpose them to their own circumstances and transform the *experience of work* in their sphere of influence.

Let me tell you a little about myself. I began my education as a Registered Nurse, then earned a BS in Psychology and an MS in Health Care Administration. Later, I attended the Program for State and Local Leaders at the JFK School of Government, Harvard University and received a certificate in Leading Organizations to Health[1]. I was honored with three Presidential Rank Awards, am a Fellow in the American College of Healthcare Executives (FACHE) and have been a Lay Associate of the Sisters of the Sorrowful Mother for 30 years. An eclectic mix of credentials, and not something I volunteer easily, except as a basis of legitimacy for my views and to claim some credibility.

I was introduced to Servant Leadership in the 1970's as a nurse at St. Vincent Health Center in Erie, PA. They actually practiced what they preached! It was my first experience with an employer who understood and applied Robert Greenleaf's principles. While the idea of Servant Leadership has been around for millennia, often attached to religious texts, I learned to admire Greenleaf's conceptualization of a practical leadership model that works for both people and companies. Greenleaf's Servant Leadership seemed to offer a pragmatic basis for the "touchy-feely" facets of management that are often discounted but are truly foundational. Greenleaf did not propose his model of leadership because it was a nice way to run a business, but because it was effective.

Early in my days as an RN, I developed an interest in moving up the private sector career ladder—not for reasons of pay or prestige, but because I could influence the care of patients and the well-being of staff. I soon found myself in middle and upper management positions in nursing and then in hospital administration, moving my family from Pennsylvania to New Jersey, Ohio, Wyoming, Wisconsin and Michigan in the

---

1   Thank you, Tony Suchman

process. In 1987 the Governor of Wisconsin appointed me to administer the five-facility State Hospital system.

In 1995 I became intrigued by Dr. Kenneth Kizer's revolutionary vision for the Veterans Health Administration and was subsequently hired to lead a region or VISN (Veterans Integrated Service Network), which encompassed policy, budget and operational oversight of 8 VA Medical Centers and 30 Community Based Outpatient Clinics across 3 states, with almost 10,000 employees, and a budget of just under $1 billion.

The VA position also demanded leadership roles on national committees, boards and task forces. Between my VISN duties and system-wide committees including Human Resources, Customer Service, Patient-Centered Care and others, I was exposed to a wide variety of participants and stakeholders, leadership and communication styles, values and priorities. Navigating a course through that variability in a way that both achieved results and respected all involved was my principal ambition. Finding and modeling that course became my passion.

Working for the government is quite a leap from private sector health care. In private enterprise there is considerably more executive flexibility and discretion, generally less scrutiny and visibility. Decisions can be made and implemented more expeditiously. The same situations which cause scathing media coverage for public institutions are barely remarked upon in private facilities. In Wisconsin, I was responsible to the Governor and in regular contact with the State Legislature. As a Senior Executive (SES) with the Department of Veterans Affairs, the United States Congress was my Board of Directors.

Even (maybe especially) in my government roles, I rigorously sought to remain apolitical (political with a capital P), although many aspects of the jobs were distinctly political and conspicuously hierarchical. Those attributes are seldom conducive to a flourishing work environment where employees are given the latitude to think, innovate, discern, contribute and grow, or to form constructive relationships with colleagues and caring relationships with customers.

To be fair, all relationships are political (political with a small p) and hierarchy doesn't just happen in government. Many contemporary organizations are top-down, often those which hold authoritarian points of view. We also tend to assign hierarchical status based on educational credentials, degrees of responsibility or prestige of position. This can have disastrous results in a multi-disciplinary health care team, for example, when a housekeeper who has an idea for improved infection control is too intimidated to present it to the physician… Or when a front-line supervisor knows that a new policy is flawed, but is hesitant to suggest an adjustment… Or when a surgeon is about to operate on the wrong leg and a demoralized nurse keeps quiet... Or when a union member fails to report a potential safety hazard because it's not his job… And on and on and on.

Hierarchy in itself is a neutral system, and can even be positive. It's helpful to know who is in charge of what and where we fit in the scheme of things. The danger in hierarchy is in the interpretation of it by those at the top, and the perception of it by everyone else. A consultant acquaintance calls the dark side of the management pyramid "hierarchicalness."[2] Greenleaf and others change the conversation altogether by turning the pyramid upside-down. To help counteract the effects of "hierarchicalness," I taught assertiveness skills to employee groups throughout the state facilities and later to the community. Some thought it strange (even irrational!) that a boss would teach staff how to say "No," to disagree, to speak up, to stop the line. I will admit this approach sometimes made my job harder, but its success in team performance and patient outcomes could not be disputed.

---

2   Thank you, Kevin Vigilante.

During my 13 years as a VISN Director, I became increasingly sensitive to the degree of incivility, apathy and learned helplessness that is sometimes encountered in political and hierarchical organizations. Those characteristics trickle down from top management, whether intentionally or not, to middle- and first-level managers, front-line staff and ultimately show up in attitudes toward patients or consumers. Hear this: I believe that as a whole, public health care employees work the hardest, do tasks many of us would eschew, are more dedicated to mission and service, for less pay and little recognition. But government rules and hierarchy have a chilling effect upon engagement, empowerment, prudent risk-taking and self-sufficiency.

And so, while VISN operations were my primary responsibility, my colleagues and I developed an initiative we called CREW: Civility, Respect and Engagement in the Workplace, to help build those skills into the Veterans Health Administration, one workgroup at a time. To our great satisfaction, CREW has now touched almost 1400 VHA workgroups, has been endorsed by The Joint Commission (the key health care accrediting body), and adopted by health, government and academic organizations in the United States, Canada, Japan.

My venture into CREW turned out to be more than a brief diversion: it culminated in a change of direction. When VHA created the new position of Director of Organizational Health, I accepted the role. For the last eight years of my VA career, I worked with psychologists, researchers and other professionals in VA's National Center for Organization Development (NCOD). NCOD acts as the organization's coach and conscience, cultivating senior leaders, nurturing productive teams, building healthier workplaces and inspiring a culture of accountability and service. My affiliation with NCOD offered a platform to further VA's familiarity with and commitment to Servant Leadership.

One of my favorite notions is that "we're all leaders, all the time." This is not a frequent Servant Leadership quote, but I believe it is one of the most profound and far-reaching. On the occasions when I teach Servant Leadership to employee groups, several things invariably happen. Supervisors in the audience begin to squirm. Rank and file staff whisper to each other that they wish their supervisors were present. In fact, if you're reading this and thinking right now about the person you report to, listen up!

No matter what your title or where you reside on the organizational chart, *each of us is called to be a leader*. We can lead at work, at home, in the community. We may be thought leaders, team leaders, leaders in a church or club; teachers, coaches or mentors; models of good work ethic, respectful behavior, process improvement, compassion. The opportunities are endless. So while many Servant Leader texts speak only to those in formal positions of authority, this volume is not limited to official leaders: it is also relevant for people at any level of the organization, whatever that organization may be. Our companies and our world today cannot afford to let *anyone* just "sit it out." *We're all leaders, all the time.* No one gets a pass.

When I recall my first exposure to Servant Leadership, I am grateful for the introduction. All my work experiences were not like St. Vincent Health Center, but each taught me something. In many cases the worst examples of leadership provided epiphanies about how I would or would not define my own leadership style. Over time I have come to think of the best examples as *the nobler side of leadership,* and to label the practices that affirm them *Humanagement.*

In the pages ahead, I describe some of the people and companies that provided those teaching moments. In particular, I share the story of the Veterans Health Administration's journey toward Servant Leadership. We will explore ideas and practices that have framed my leadership philosophy, with recurring themes about healthy organizations, organizational culture and their inherent connections. Each chapter opens and closes with "All Things Connected," short commentaries adapted from my writings to VHA staff over the last 20 years.

To make the text more interactive, you will note "Reality Checks ✓ " throughout. These ask you to think more deeply about your own experience or translate the concept to your own setting. I'll also provide activities and tools that can be used individually or with a group to help you understand or develop the concept more fully. The tools can be incorporated into your personal action planning.

There are no passengers on Spaceship Earth. We are all CREW ...

– Marshall McCluhan

Whatever else it is, Servant Leadership is not a fad or a flavor of the month, it's not easy to implement and it can't be feigned. It is by necessity consistent and must be authentic. It's a mission, an obsession and a lifelong commitment. When people ask me if I practice Servant Leadership, I say, "Yes...I practice and I practice and I practice!"

All Things Connected...

Life is art. Work is the canvas on which we display our souls.

As we learn to appreciate a good painting, we understand it at several levels. We can walk through a gallery and enjoy a well-wrought picture of a landscape, a fine portrait or a mind-altering modern masterpiece for just what it is. Often the simple pleasure of seeing what is in front of us is enough.

But sometimes there's more going on beneath the surface. I'm a fan of hidden-object puzzles where, embedded within a picture, are all sorts of items waiting for discovery. It's necessary to squint or peer off-center to find the hidden images. We are at risk of not seeing them unless we explicitly search for them.

As I contemplate the brushstroke of a Rembrandt, the palette of a Vermeer or the eccentricity of a Bosch, I'm intrigued by the intricacy of what is behind the scenes. Those observations shape how we perceive and react to the painting itself. If we don't know enough to look for the hidden, there's no chance we'll find it.

So we *see* a work of art at an observable level, and we *think* about it at an analytical level. But perhaps the artist most hoped we would *feel* it at a sublime level. How does it affect our senses? What is the impression or "field" it creates? Does it lift us from the mundane? What is its story? How do we absorb it from an ethereal perspective? Does it produce an epiphanal moment? Are we better for having experienced it?

You are no less a work of art. I can choose to relate to you as I encounter you every day, with courtesy and civility—no more, no less. I can judge you by your appearance, your status, my own personal biases and our history together. I can regard you through an *exterior* lens.

Or I might decide to dig deeper, identify what makes you tick, recognize your multi-dimensional nature, uncover your buried treasures. I may have to squint or peer off-center, but unless I alter my vantage point, I won't know what treasures are there to find. We see what we expect and want to see. I can regard you through an *interior* lens.

Better yet, I might transcend what I see and think, and reflect on my impression of you.

Everyone creates an energy or "field" that reveals our principles, priorities and values. It emanates from us.

Our reputation as honorable or opportunistic, serving or self-centered, kind or harsh, is the manifestation of that field. It is how others "know" us.

What is the ethos or field that surrounds you?

I can choose to rise above the irritations and annoyances that wound our relationship and conceal the authentic you. I can elect to be mindful of the message "above the line," and regard you through a *superior* lens.

I admire the Sanskrit expression *Namaste*: "the sacred in me greets the sacred in you." Far more than a New Age sentiment, this is a profound declaration of our inherent worth.

We can choose to interact from our surface selves, our analytical selves or our higher selves.

This is not a lesson in art appreciation: it is a reminder that, even in the madness and mess of the workplace, we can resolve to reach that greater consciousness which connects us all.

...All Things Connected

Mall Map:

You Are Here

You are here → **Front Line Staff**

Mid-Level Manager

You are here →

Executive

← You are here

✑ Instructions ✐

When we are looking for direction at a large shopping center, we seek out the Mall Map to determine where we are. *You Are Here* is your location in the context of the stores around you. The *You Are Here* designation moves as you move around the mall, but always places you in spatial proximity to other landmarks.

Your place in the organization can change in much the same way. How you demonstrate leadership may depend on your relative position and level of authority. Keeping in mind that *we're all leaders, all the time,* what does your leadership look like to others when you are:

- Front-line staff (those who work directly with the customer)
- A middle manager
- An executive

By what actions will your colleagues identify you as a leader, as a Servant Leader?

Here are some examples of things you might do so your colleagues see you as a Servant Leader:

FRONT-LINE

- Offer to help other team members
- Take a moment to say good morning or ask how someone is
- Smile
- Open a door for a patient or co-worker
- Introduce yourself to new associates
- Offer an idea to improve the work you do

MID-LEVEL

- Communicate honestly/respectfully, both upwards and downwards in authority
- Give developmental opportunities to staff
- Welcome feedback, even when it isn't good news
- Keep staff informed about the "big picture" and how they fit into it
- Compliment good work
- Be a coach, not a critic

- Serve a snack to the night shift
- Model Servant Leadership in your language (verbal and written)
- Share credit for accomplishments
- Publicly recognize Servant Leader behavior at all levels
- Solicit suggestions from staff and customers
- Model what's right, not what's expedient

❧ Discussion ❦

This activity can be used individually or in small groups. If done in a group, try to include people at all three levels of the Mall Map pictured above. Are the actions different in each level? Do any of the actions in the other levels surprise you?

While many of the actions you list may be things you do almost unconsciously, take a moment to think about them *intentionally*.

Are there additional things you can do to demonstrate your leadership where you are right now on the Mall Map? How might someone demonstrate leadership at other levels?

Consider the statement, "You're not a Servant Leader until others say you are." What does this mean? How might this statement alter your leadership behaviors?

❧ Chapter References ❦

Greenleaf, R. K. (1970). *The Servant as Leader*. Atlanta, GA: The Greenleaf Center for Servant Leadership.

Jennings, K. and Stahl-Wert, J. (2004). *The Serving Leader*. San Francisco, CA: Berrett-Koehler.

Keith, K. M. (2010). *Questions and Answers about Servant Leadership*. Westfield, IN: Greenleaf Center for Servant Leadership.

McCluhan, M., www.brainyquote.com

Patrnchak, J. M. (2016). *The Engaged Enterprise*. Atlanta, GA: Greenleaf Center for Servant Leadership.

Spears, L. (1998). *Insights into Leadership: Service, Stewardship, Spirit and Servant Leadership*. New York: Wiley.

CHAPTER TWO

Organizational Health & Culture

All Things Connected...

Do you remember the children's story of *Pollyanna*? Pollyanna is an orphan taken in by her reclusive aunt. Despite a difficult life, she always looks for the positive; searches for the best in people. Conversely, her aunt always expects the worst and has a low estimation of human nature.

Events escalate until Pollyanna's brightness is finally extinguished by the persistent negativity around her. With her light gone, family and townsfolk acknowledge how empty their lives have become. Of course there's a happy ending when the community "culture" shifts to adopt Pollyanna's optimism.

It has always baffled me to hear the derisive tone associated with "being a Pollyanna." What does it say about a society where cynicism has higher value than idealism? Where a cheerful, hopeful approach is seen as unrealistic or *flaky*? Where caring is overridden by judging? Where learning about someone's failure is more satisfying than hearing of their success? Where we seek to define our separateness more than our connection?

Sociologists blame our disillusionment on the state of politics, corporations and the economy. Since workplaces are a microcosm of the larger culture, it's no surprise that those attitudes trickle down.

It's easy to become distrustful of those who have more power, who work in unfamiliar environments or hold different views. It's common to suspect their motives, question their intentions, become defensive or push back. Sometimes those reactions are warranted. Almost always, at some level of consciousness, they are an attempt to redress the balance of power.

One way to deal with those feelings is to compartmentalize them, but beware of rationalizations for being less than our higher selves. "It's just business," or "No margin, no mission," may be clues that we've disconnected who we think we need to be from who we really are. Any time we suspend our values to get over a bump in the road, our internal alarms should go off.

We are faced daily with life's tough realities, things we don't like, events beyond our control, even pain. It's not unnatural to become jaded, frustrated, demoralized. But perhaps there has never been a time that we needed Pollyannas more.

Let's not forget among our heroes those Pollyannas who, in the face of a dim reality, create their own reality; who are quick to smile, ready to help, slow to anger, disposed to listen, and who delight in saying, "Yes!" Who don't write off what seems impossible, but ask how to make it possible. Who shape their environment instead of being shaped by it. Who dig deep to uncover opportunities, even when they're buried in the muck. Who lead culture change within their sphere of influence, no matter how small or large that sphere may be. Who look past conflict and confrontation to glimpse the radiance of our humanity.

"Pollyanna-ism" is not head-in-the-sand- behavior: it's a perspective of hopefulness and possibility. Being called a Pollyanna is a testament to resilience, self-actualization, character and compassion.

If you are so fortunate as to wear this label, don't protest. Say, "Thank you!" Refuse to let your light be extinguished.

... All Things Connected

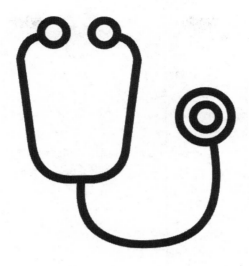

Doctor, Doctor, Give Me the News…
—Robert Palmer

M r. Womack is being evaluated for heart disease. Numerous clinical indicators are assessed to determine his risk factors and current status: blood pressure, cholesterol, diet, smoking, exercise, weight and family history, to name a few. The health care team gathers an array of data and, based on those data, plans targeted interventions to address Mr. Womack's condition. No one would tell Mr. Womack that if he loses weight he can continue to smoke. No one would suggest that if he takes his lipid medication he can eat all the fatty foods he likes. All the relevant factors are viewed in concert, not in isolation. Through his course of care new indicators may become relevant, new tests available, new interventions discovered. Mr. Womack's treatment is not static: it is adjusted and adapted as new evidence emerges. The goal for this patient is not just improved blood pressure or lab results, but *comprehensive cardiac health.*

Organizations are like people. They can be healthy or ailing and even moribund. An organization's state of health affects its employees, customers, processes, reputation and bottom line. Numerous institutional indicators are assessed to determine the risk factors and current status of the organization: customer satisfaction, employee satisfaction, labor/ management relations, diversity climate, safety data, recruitment and retention figures, financial and quality monitors and others. The leadership team gathers an array of data and, based on those data, plans targeted interventions to address the organization's condition. No one would suggest that the company focus on quality and disregard the budget. No one would pour dollars into recruiting staff, but ignore efforts to retain them. All the relevant factors are viewed in concert, not in isolation. Through the organization's course of care new indicators may become relevant, new measures available, new interventions undertaken. Treatment is not static: it is adjusted and adapted as new evidence emerges. The goal for this business is not just improved cash flow or satisfaction scores, but *comprehensive Organizational Health.*

A person in pain does not only feel the localized effects of that pain: it impacts their sleep, appetite, mobility, energy, productivity, mood, etc. Organizations in pain cannot isolate its effects either: it seeps into their ethics, agility, relationships, ability to attract talent, customer loyalty and culture.

HEALTH—MIND, BODY AND SPIRIT

Health is not simply the absence of disease. Holistically healthy individuals reflect physical, mental, spiritual and social well-being. When holistic principles are applied to organizations (Bruhn, 2001):

- The BODY refers to the structure, design, uses of power, communication processes and distribution of work.

- The MIND denotes underlying beliefs, goals, how policies are implemented, how conflict is handled, how people are treated and how the organization learns.

- The SPIRIT is its core or heart—its values, what makes it vibrant and gives it vigor.

Healthy organizations, like healthy individuals, don't just happen: we have to work at making it so. Improving Organizational Health demands honest self-assessment, constant fine-tuning, candid yet caring conversations and attention to relationships.

When a work unit is off-balance, other work units are disturbed as well. When one part of the organization is out of alignment, the entire system suffers. Timely intervention can remedy a critical or chronic condition.

NURTURING WORKPLACE SUCCESS

In VHA we say that *healthy organizations are places where employees want to work and patients/Veterans want to receive care.* If you are not in a health care setting, translate that into terms that are meaningful for you. Employees and customers (whatever you would call your "customers") are your pivot points of success, and the element of choice should be central to your thinking. Make no mistake: employees and customers can go elsewhere, even if they seem like a captive audience.

All of us interact with a variety of organizations on a daily basis. Organizations touch many aspects of our life experience. We are consumers, patrons, students, staff, church-goers and members of professional, social and charitable associations. Organizations can be rigid, bureaucratic and user-hostile or supportive, nourishing and customer-centered. Most of us spend at least one third of our time in organizational work environments. Imagine the potential and positive impact of a healthy organization!

Organizational Health can be defined as a state of systemic well-being that nurtures success in complex and chaotic organizations. (Are there any contemporary organizations that are not complex and chaotic?!) Organizational Health is not just one more thing to do: it's the way we do everything. In Gandhi's words, "the end is inherent in the means." Healthy organizations outperform others in service, quality, safety, ethics, efficiency and satisfaction. They are incubators of innovation and transformation. *Healthy organizations are foundation, not fluff.* They:

- ✓ Afford employees the security and the freedom to excel, within the framework of a clear mission and consistent corporate values

- ✓ Provide a safe environment in which to take reasonable risks, make reasoned judgments, act creatively and thrive on challenge and change

- ✓ Rely on thinking, caring employees who work respectfully as part of a team, are fully engaged, continuously improve and innovate, understand their personal link to the mission, are passionate about service and are committed to personal growth

Healthy places to work demonstrate what a colleague of mine calls "organizational ecology."[3]

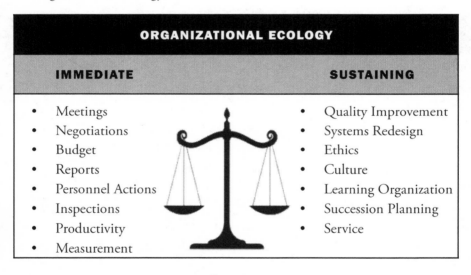

ORGANIZATIONAL ECOLOGY

IMMEDIATE	SUSTAINING
• Meetings	• Quality Improvement
• Negotiations	• Systems Redesign
• Budget	• Ethics
• Reports	• Culture
• Personnel Actions	• Learning Organization
• Inspections	• Succession Planning
• Productivity	• Service
• Measurement	

FIGURE 1

Figure 1 illustrates the equilibrium between taking care of immediate tasks and concerns and building systems that strengthen and sustain the organization over time, that is, the balance of reactive leadership and proactive leadership. When I walk into my workplace each day, I am thinking about the immediate tasks, the pressing assignments on my plate, and wondering what unanticipated events might arise.

---

3   Thank you, Jerry Born.

But as I consider *what* I'll be doing, I need to reflect on *how* I'll be doing it. Am I reinforcing the desired culture? Am I incorporating learning from the past? Am I modeling ethical decision-making? Am I cutting corners or making improvements?

Leaders in healthy organizations keep the ecological scale in mind and check its balance on a regular basis. This is about leaving the organization in a better state than you found it, holding the organization in trust. This is the meaning of *stewardship*.

REALITY CHECK ✓

In your work environment, what things would
you place on the two sides of the Ecology Scale?
How would you ensure it stays in balance?

A healthy organization has parameters: not the rule-bound strictness of many bureaucracies, but limits that provide guidance for safe risk-taking and prudent decision-making and offer a comfort zone for stakeholders. While limits are usually thought of as horizontal (how far can I go?), in a healthy organization, they are also vertical. Servant Leaders delineate *and guard* a cultural floor and a ceiling.

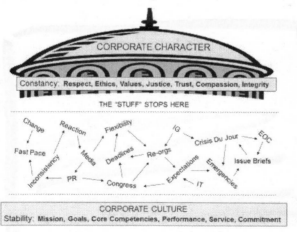

FIGURE 2

In VHA, the floor denotes our foundation: our mission, goals, competencies and commitment to service. This is where stability lies. A mission is the bedrock of a company's structure, its reason for being. It's the shared and often-invoked ideology that attracts people to the organization and keeps them there. It is the fundamental source of *corporate culture*.

Conversely, the ceiling signifies our *corporate character*, how we are known, the values we profess: integrity, compassion, advocacy, respect, excellence, ethics and justice. These values form the thread of constancy that is woven throughout the organization's consciousness, the code and custom by which the mission is fulfilled.

Figure 2 depicts these important upper and lower parameters, but we should also observe the space in between. The words listed here signify tasks and events that fill our workdays, and the arrows show that they are flying in all directions. Our days are rife with routines and crises; they are largely unpredictable. They often seem to swirl and escalate in ways that threaten to overwhelm us.

In healthy organizations, leaders understand the vulnerabilities of an overwhelmed work force and strategically "keep a lid" on things. These are the leaders who draw a *line in the sky*, who say, "Enough!," who hold the mission and the values sacrosanct, who make decisions within the framework of those values even when it's not the popular wisdom, who support their employees even in the face of personal risk.

I recall times in my career when it would have been so much easier to let that line slide. Many years ago I was asked to falsify a staffing roster in order to pass a state inspection. When I refused, my job, my home and my reputation were threatened. Another time pressure was exerted on me to make a sizable donation to a political campaign supported by my employer. "This is not the time or place for your ethics," I was told. "This is exactly the time and place," I responded. Thankfully, the implied threat was not carried out. Principles and ethics have little merit if they are compromised for expedience or when the going gets rough.

Leaders have a set of obligations to their employees. Employees have a set of obligations to their employers. *A healthy organization is a compact between these various workers and the workplace.*

CULTURE AND TRANSFORMATION

So what exactly is *culture*? Cameron and Quinn (2011) define culture as the taken-for-granted values, assumptions and expectations that characterize organizations and their members. Corporate culture is the heart and the felt personality of the organization. Leaders spend a great deal of time planning strategy, but without attention to the underlying culture, those strategies are often built on sand. Healthy organizations tend to their culture *first*.

Culture happens by intention or default. Whether it is developed with foresight and purpose or left to chance, *there is always a culture*, and in great part the leader determines what it will be. Physicist Rupert Sheldrake (2016) speculates about "fields" of culture within an organization. Much as we accept the existence of electromagnetic and gravitational fields, even though we can't see them, he proposes that culture "fields" are every bit as real.

Let me give an example. I used to shop in a store where soft classical music was playing, the air was lightly perfumed, the clothing wrapped carefully in tissue paper, the clerks helpful, but not overbearing. The "field" there echoed old-fashioned respect, a slower pace, pampering and service. I was drawn to that store not just for the shopping but for the experience as well.

And then there was the doctor's office where a gentle waterfall trickled in the waiting room, complementary therapies were available, staff related to patients with warmth and personal interest, there was no sense of being rushed or being "just a number" and clinicians really listened. The "field" there was one of well-being, peacefulness, privacy and partnership.

I suggest that fields reflect the organization's dominant values in both measurable and sensory ways. Imagine fields of service or empowerment or justice or compassion! We can sense the field around us, which then stimulates us to perpetuate it. Leaders who both *talk* and *walk* an organization's desired characteristics and behaviors, consistently and visibly, generate an ethos or a field that replicates itself at all levels and permeates the workplace.

Einstein posited that the most important decision we make is whether we believe we live in a friendly or hostile universe, and that the universe responds to this belief. In that case, we literally create the work environments we choose to believe in.

As a director of health care systems for more than 25 years, I often made visits to the Medical Centers and clinics within my jurisdiction. The personalities of these sites were almost palpable. At one hospital, for example, the visit would be very formal. A delegation of managers would meet me at the door. Others would scuttle away. There would be a rigid itinerary. As we moved from one location to another, I would hear a secretary calling over to the next area: "She just left the lobby; she's on her way to 2 North." People were stiff and on their best behavior. I was often steered away from trouble spots and discouraged from speaking directly to Veterans and staff.

Contrast this with my experience at another hospital where my visit was received as business as usual. There was an atmosphere of warmth and welcome. The leadership team had an itinerary, but modified it as we went along. I was asked what I wanted to see. Staff stopped to talk with me along the way. They were eager to show their accomplishments and share their ideas. I was given unescorted time where I could wander about freely, asking Veterans about their care. Employees around me seemed to be relaxed and enjoying their work.

The culture in these hospitals was tangible. Staff learn the culture not only by hearing the official pitch (a necessary component), but also by watching how closely that pitch is aligned with the way things are actually done. They monitor:

- How decisions are made
- How problems are resolved
- How conflict is handled (or allowed to fester)
- How information is shared
- How bad news is received
- What behavior is modeled
- What behavior is rewarded

Because *all things are connected*, the culture created at the top invariably spills over into employees' perceptions of the workplace, organizational performance and outcomes and customers' opinions and approval (NCOD).

If your organization is like most, top management demands culture change by tomorrow. Resist! Culture change is a process: it is built on behaviors, not on rhetoric. It takes time to crystalize. While some forward movement should be noticeable along the way, it may take a few years to claim success. A leader can achieve some results by fiat, but what happens when that leader leaves? We cannot declare victory until the culture is woven into the fabric of the organization.

THE ORGANIZATIONAL HEALTH UMBRELLA

Early in my tenure as Director of Organizational Health, it became apparent that one person could only do so much. At the beginning, I was a one-person program with no discretionary budget (a far cry from the human and financial resources available to me as VISN Director!) My "adoption" by NCOD (VHA's National Center for Organization Development) helped to rectify that.

As Organizational Health initiatives surged in popularity, dedicated staff were brought on board to support them. Nevertheless, there was always an awareness of being a "prophet in one's own land," a kind of isolation I soon found was a shared experience. We all travel lighter with companions on the journey, and so we search for avenues of connection.

THE ORGANIZATIONAL HEALTH COMMUNITY

As I crossed the country teaching VA groups about civility, Servant Leadership and other topics commonly considered "soft," I anticipated pushback and resistance. Many leaders had staked their territory years ago and struggled with fresh approaches. These people were comfortable with the traditional "hard skills" and that was what the system traditionally rewarded. But we were bent on creating some new traditions.

What I was not prepared for was the resonance of these themes to so many others, across the organizational strata. How frequently participants would shyly approach, hungry for more information! How often they would tell me they "got it," but that their supervisors didn't! How many expressed that they, too, felt like lone voices in the wilderness! Healthy organizations are grounded in healthy individuals, but it is not enough to capture hearts and minds, one person at a time. It is necessary to forge linkages, develop synergies and build community.

And so I came to realize that we are all alone in this *together*.

ORGANIZATIONAL SYNERGY

In addition to finding individuals of like minds, I quickly discovered programs that shared the philosophy of Organizational Health. I am reminded of the story of the elephant and the blind man: where one touches the elephant determines how one sees it (a trunk? a tiny tail? enormous feet?).

And so it is in the work world: whether one intersects it though ethics, systems redesign, civility, customer service, safety, diversity, learning or leadership programs, it's all Organizational Health. It takes a myriad of initiatives with their own unique focus to produce a whole and healthy enterprise.

Organizational Health in VA

FIGURE 3

The Umbrella in Figure 3 became VHA's symbol of Organizational Health. It represents those programs and initiatives that support and sustain a healthy organization, from their particular vantage point. They do not report to Organizational Health or any central structure, but are dispersed throughout and appreciate their casual synergy. It soon became a badge of honor for a program logo to be included under the Organizational Health Umbrella!

REALITY CHECK ✓

In your organization, what programs would you include
under your Organizational Health Umbrella?

ORGANIZATIONAL HEALTH COUNCILS— JUST ANOTHER MEETING?

A few years ago, we conjectured that the informal associations of programs under the Umbrella could be enhanced by some official recognition and structure. The reality is that many local programs, like those under the Umbrella, are one- or two-person operations. Ironically, they exert a broad scope of influence and responsibility across the Medical Center. These were small programs with a big impact. No one wants yet another committee, especially if it does not add value to the work. But what if these program managers convened in a forum that supported and synergized their efforts? What if they collectively represented the face of a healthy organization?

Those questions led VHA's National Center for Organization Development (NCOD) to wonder if Medical Centers and VISNs could improve their outcomes and their culture by establishing Organizational Health Councils. To that end, 142 VHA care sites were polled, inquiring whether they had such a Council. Many of the respondents acknowledged a committee that addressed one or more aspects of Organizational

Health such as workforce development, employee satisfaction or customer service. But a striking observation of the poll was the variability across the country: only a handful of sites declared any sort of integrated or systemic forum (Organizational Health, 2013).

Over time, several factors were understood to maximize the effectiveness of Organizational Health Councils:

✓ **Membership**

Having the right mix of program leads. In VHA, that could include coordinators of patient centered care, CREW (Civility, Respect and Engagement in the Workplace), diversity/equal opportunity; Veteran advocates, Chief Learning Officers; contacts for employee wellness, safety, ethics, redesign and other initiatives. These are people who rarely work together, but whose areas of responsibility are congruent.

✓ **Authority/Reporting Relationship/Structure**

The Council should be designated as an advisory or consultative body, reporting to and having a champion in top management, and a home in the leadership or governance structure. It should be formally charged and chartered. While it is not recommended that it hold decision-making authority, the proximity to the C-Suite gives the Council standing and ensures it will be taken seriously.

✓ **Function**

The Council's perspective should be at "30,000 feet," a big picture perspective. Since the programs are traditionally independent from each other, the Council provides an opportunity to find common ground, synthesize and synergize their efforts and identify areas of overlap and duplication. It may draft action plans, propose measures to enhance a healthy workplace, oversee performance and satisfaction survey data, emphasize connections between programs and orchestrate their efforts.

In just a few years, the number of Organizational Health Councils in VHA increased almost 300%. The wisdom of an Organizational Health Council is that it is greater than the sum of its parts.

TRANSFORMATION IN A HEALTHY ORGANIZATION

Transformation has become a buzzword in many organizations. We make changes to people and processes all the time, but that is not transformation. Renovation, conversion, revolution and metamorphosis are synonyms for transformation. This is not superficial change, playing around the edges. Transformational change is neither transactional (e.g., exchanging one process for another), translational (e.g., reinterpreting a process) nor transitional (e.g., temporary use of a process; a placeholder). Transformational organizations challenge us to raise the bar, climb to the next level, engage in astonishing ways, forge radical new connections and transcend our own self-interests to accomplish something far greater.

As Director, it was necessary for me to design the Organizational Health program out of whole cloth, to build it from the ground up. To facilitate a vision, devise a thoughtful blueprint and most coherently focus my work, I developed an aspirational model of the Transformational Workplace.

Transformational Workplace

Patient Centered Care, Customer Service
Safe, Timely, Quality Outcomes

Serving the Veteran

Veteran-Centric

Serving the Employee

Serving the Organization

CREW (Civility)
Systems Redesign
Effective Teams

Employee Engagement

Leadership

Integrated Ethics
Learning Organization
Servant Leadership

FIGURE 4

35

Transformation is the epitome of culture change. The Transformational Model is the embodiment of Organizational Health's mantra: *All Things Connected.*

The transformational organization is illustrated in three essential service-driven domains:

- It is customer or patient-oriented. In VHA, priorities like patient centered care, customer service and safe/timely/quality health outcomes fall into this sphere. Veteran patients and their families are given the information and respect needed to be active partners in their own health care decisions. Health status is enriched by healing relationships with the Veteran, and by the quality of the Veteran's experience with VA. Other workplaces may substitute accessibility, response rates, rework, recidivism, consumer loyalty or other factors. The customer, however that is defined, is acknowledged as the *raison d'etre* of the organization. This sphere embraces *serving the customer.*

- It is fueled by knowledgeable, engaged and empowered employees. VHA programs in civility (CREW), systems redesign, diversity and inclusion and team effectiveness are examples relevant to this domain. Staff is educated, encouraged and expected to do whatever it takes to meet the needs of the Veteran. The environment is geared toward helping employees to be competent and confident, to feel physically and psychologically safe, to act boldly and compassionately, to find joy in their colleagues and their work. In other organizations, employee wellness and satisfaction, career development, incentive programs and other factors could also be included here. This sphere supports *serving the employee.*

- It is guided by principled and progressive leadership. In VHA, initiatives centered around integrated ethics, systemic learning, performance measurement, executive coaching and Servant Leadership reside in this sphere. That these leaders are skilled in the hard management disciplines, that they act within the confines of the law, are givens. They go beyond the basics: they are moral and participative decision-makers; they provide the tools and resources to do the job, then trust their people to do it; they practice accountability but not micromanagement. These leaders do the right things for the right reasons at the right time; they listen deeply and communicate transparently. They inspire followership. If these traits sound suspiciously like Servant Leadership, it's because they are. I have not found a better leadership model for a transformational organization. This sphere is about *serving the organization*.

Whatever your starting point on the Transformational Model, the connections are obvious: an organization requires principled and progressive leaders...to support engaged and empowered employees...who then provide exceptional, customer-centric service. Efforts in the three domains must be simultaneous, not sequential.

A leader cannot say, "This week I'll work on satisfying my customers and I'll think about my employees in the spring," or "I'll worry about ethics when I've met my performance goals." Serving the customer, serving the employee and serving the organization are interdependent in nature. In a transformational organization, failure in any of the spheres is not an option.

Take-Aways from the Transformational Model

✓ **Customer-Centric**
- Nothing about me without me: building systems and processes around the customer
- Establish a consistent "line of sight" from the boardroom to the bedside
- The customer is the final arbiter of value

✓ **Employee Engagement**

- Create an environment that nurtures both risk-taking and accountability
- Empower employees to be actively engaged and connected to the mission
- Relationships are fundamental

✓ **Servant Leadership**

- Leaders build and sustain a culture of service
- We're all leaders, all the time

THE IMPERATIVE OF A HEALTHY ORGANIZATION

If at this point in the narrative, healthy organizations sound like a lot of trouble, you've been paying attention! They are, and they are worth it. In my grandfather's day, he expected an autocratic boss at the top of an impenetrable hierarchy. He did not expect to be consulted about decisions that would affect him. He was expected to toe the line, even if that meant long hours in a questionably safe environment. The quality of his output was important, but his relationship with co-workers and his family obligations were of little interest to the company. He was paid fairly and, if he faithfully produced over the decades, he would receive a pension and a gold watch to mark his retirement. The times, the work norms and the corporate culture mirrored a more inhibited, conservative frame of reference.

For most of us, that is no longer acceptable.

Prompted by global dynamics, personal beliefs and generational paradigms, the attitudes, objectives and expectations of the workforce have changed. The compact between the organization and the employee has been redefined. Research has illuminated the nexus of leadership, internal and external customer satisfaction and the bottom line. Whichever reason resonates with your company, whatever motivates your institution to join the parade, almost doesn't matter. The return on investment for a healthy organization is conclusive.

Organizational Health does not guarantee there won't be daunting problems, periodic belt tightening, grievances or complaints. It does, however, establish an environment that is more likely to prevent or mitigate those occurrences. Healthy organizations still have to fire and discipline, rectify public blunders and weather crises. But they do it in a way that safeguards truth-telling and honors our common humanity.

My simple visual of a Healthy Organization looks like this:

A healthy organization is like a house built on rock. It:

- Provides a framework for quality, cost, service, safety, diversity, accountability
- Offers a pathway for recruitment, retention and succession planning
- Is a conduit for ethical decision-making
- Cultivates a satisfied, engaged workforce

All sheltered by an overarching culture of Servant Leadership,
And culminating in organizational excellence.

Organizational Health is foundation, not fluff!

All Things Connected...

The term "culture" is used a lot these days. Organizational culture is the environment we share by virtue of working in the same system.

Culture is the personality of the organization. It is the composite values, principles, customs and behaviors that have become the norm with time and repetition. It's how things are really done.

There is a feel to an office or work unit that embraces customer service; stress and tension between co-workers can be sensed; there's a certain vibe when staff are proud of their performance and another when they just want the workday to be over.

Some places feel welcoming to visitors; others are more closed. Some convey an aura of arrogance or paternalism, others a mood of partnership. It's easy to pick up when people are fearful or they're comfortable having fun on the job.

There are many indicators of a positive organizational culture: being greeted with a smile, stray trash is picked up, an absence of long waiting lines, a visitor who's lost is helped, staff from other departments call each other by name, accessibility of administrative offices, easy collaboration between disciplines, visible display of performance data.

Culture encompasses the attitudes, actions and atmosphere at work, and determines how we are perceived outside the walls of our workplace.

Culture is a big tent:

- In a culture of resistance, new ideas are challenged, despite their logic

- In a culture of accountability, we trust each other's judgment

- In an ethical culture, we do the right thing, even when no one is looking

- In a culture of service, relationships come first, even on a bad day

- In a rigid culture, we live by rules, not common sense or compassion

- In a culture of excellence, we continually reinvent

- In a team culture, people seek out different points of view

- In a culture of silence, information is withheld

- In a we-they culture, allegiances are formed by creating a common enemy

- In a culture of Servant Leadership, supervisors eliminate barriers and get out of the way

In which of these cultures would you rather work?

In healthy organizations, culture is deliberate and planned; in others, it's allowed to "metastasize" on its own. But there is *always* a culture. And while managers set the cultural tone, we're all leaders in influencing and improving the culture.

The state of our cultural health can be experienced and it can be measured. A flourishing organizational culture wraps itself around the concrete tasks of the workday, the problems and grievances, the "difficult" patient or customer, the contrary co-worker, the achievements and successes. It gently shapes how we perceive them and how we choose to handle them.

Culture cannot be concealed. It manifests in all our relationships, in our decisions, policies and choices, in what we reward and what we tolerate, in our generosity of spirit. At its essence, culture reveals the *heart of the organization.*

...All Things Connected

TOOLBOX ACTIVITY:
The Organizational Health Compact

Attribute	What you should expect from a healthy organization	What a healthy organization should expect from you	Alignment with core values
Respect			
Engagement			
Processes			
Innovation			
Dialogue			
Recognition			
Ethics			
Teamwork			
Professional Development			
Mission			

❧ Instructions ❧

Work is a compact or covenant between the employer and the employee. Sometimes the attributes of the compact are made clear by policy or practice. Often what seems clear in policy is muddied by "the way we really do things here": the silent culture of the organization.

Healthy workplaces are more likely to be explicit and engage in dialog about mutual expectations. Job fit/job congruence is important. It's to the supervisor's advantage to hire people who support the attributes of the organization: they become happy, productive, long-term employees. Workers benefit when they join organizations whose mission and values they espouse. They take satisfaction in the work and make meaningful contributions.

Look at the grid on the preceding page. Using the attributes listed on the left, complete the grid thoughtfully. If you are currently working in a healthy organization, you may respond with *what is*. If not, you can enter *what you'd like it to be*. Finally, if your organization promotes a core value related to the attribute, identify it.

❧ Discussion ❧

On your own or in a small group, consider the following:

- Are there additional attributes that are important in a healthy workplace? If so, can we agree to honor them?

- How close are the *what is* responses to the *what you'd like it to be* answers? Which attributes show the biggest gaps?

- Are some members of the organization meeting the compact more or less consistently than others?

- What can I or my group do to improve adherence to the ideal?

- How well do our behaviors align with the core values?

❧ Chapter References ❦

Belton, L. (Fall 2013) *Organizational Health Newsletter Vol. 20.*

Bruhn, J. (2001). *Trust and the Health of Organizations.* New York: Kluwer Academic/Plenum Publishers.

Cameron, K. S. and Quinn, R. E., (2011). *Diagnosing and Changing Organizational Culture.* San Francisco, CA: Jossey-Bass.

Sheldrake, R. (March 2016) www.sheldrake.org. *Morphic Resonance and Morphic Fields.*

CHAPTER THREE

*Servant Leadership
Principles & Practice*

All Things Connected...

ENRON: the poster child for a company without a conscience. The current economic horizon is replete with examples of organizations that show the face of greed and indifference. Hearing someone say, "Don't take it personally, it's just business," makes me shudder!

Why did you get into the business of health care? Why did you choose this organization? For most of us the answer is: we wanted to serve.

There is nothing evil about the business side of an organization. Clearly a Medical Center couldn't hire staff, purchase equipment, build facilities or treat patients without sound business principles and good stewardship of resources. The business aspects of any organization are critical. The problem arises when "business" is driving the bus and "customer, employee and service" are just along for the ride.

Robert Greenleaf understood this. In "The Servant as Leader," he created a business case for service. An executive at AT&T, Greenleaf grasped the link between satisfied customers, empowered employees

and superior business outcomes. (In VA we use the same business case for Civility, Respect and Engagement in the Workplace [CREW], patient centered care, a learning organization, systems redesign, etc.)

Greenleaf realized that to produce this climate, *leadership is key.* In fact, he said Servant Leaders serve first and lead second, that the critical test is: do those served become healthier, wiser, freer, more autonomous, more likely themselves to become servants?

Servant Leadership is fundamental to transformation.

So what about the flip side? Can a Servant Leader organization also be accountable? It can and it must! A service orientation is not a hall pass to skip accountability.

But let's be clear about what accountability is. It is defined as responsible, liable, answerable, obligated, duty-bound.

Unfortunately, accountability is often a euphemism for blame, scapegoating and witch hunts. This is all too often the case in political or governmental systems. When calls for accountability turn into finger-pointing frenzies, the notion becomes tainted and confusing. Such messages perpetuate anxiety, dampen creativity and chill risk-taking.

Constructive accountability can only take root in a psychologically safe environment where employees at all levels are willing to speak difficult truths, question authority, admit error.

Failures in accountability are really breaches of trust: layers of oversight are then built to bridge them.

Here's how I see it:

- Accountability is a state of mind
- Accountability motivated by fear is unproductive and unethical
- Accountability arising from stewardship and compassion is powerful
- If we do the right thing only because we are told to, we give away our personal control

- Sometimes it takes courage to go outside the system; sometimes it takes more courage to change it from within
- Leaders need to create and constantly reinforce an atmosphere of truth-telling. We have a responsibility to really listen to one another

Accountability extends to what we owe society, the organization, those we serve and each other—not because we are afraid of the consequences, but because we have clear priorities, an intrinsic calling and moral courage. Accountability and ethics happen when no one is looking. Perhaps the highest standard we can hold is the ability to look ourselves in the mirror.

Every now and then we see organizations with corrosive cultures. Maybe our own gets tarnished from time to time. Let us remember that a "virtuous" culture can never be taken for granted; it must be consistently groomed and guarded.

Servant Leadership is a platform for accountability *and* service in organizations that have caring at their core. Leading with a servant's heart is nothing less than an opportunity to love.

...All Things Connected

I once was lost, but now am found…
—Amazing Grace

Servant Leadership may be tricky to define, but we usually know it when we see it. Or the reverse: it is crystal clear when someone is *not* a Servant Leader.

Of the many supervisors I've had over the years, two stand out in stark contrast:

Leader A was fond of saying, "Rank has its privileges," or "Because I say so." Leader B quoted Michelangelo, "I saw an angel in the marble and I chiseled until I set it free."

Leader A saw his position as a means to an end. He cut corners, flaunted his authority, used people for his own advantage and kept everyone off balance. He was generous and entertaining to those he liked; those he didn't like, simply didn't exist. He created havoc in the organization for three years before moving on to more fertile ground.

Leader B viewed his position as a trust. Just being in his presence made one smile. He was known for his "stretch assignments," for always giving the confidence needed, and staff typically exceeded his expectations. On the occasions when counseling or discipline was called for, it was done with compassion and clarity, leaving the employee motivated, not demoralized. When this leader retired, he was grieved.

Servant Leadership is both a philosophy and a set of practices. Servant Leaders are persons of integrity who lead an organization to success by putting the needs of customers, employees and communities first, by sharing knowledge and power and by helping people develop and perform to their highest capacity.

The Servant Leadership movement was introduced by Robert K. Greenleaf with the publication of his essay, *The Servant as Leader*, in 1970. That Greenleaf developed his ideas from a business platform is relevant and powerful. The groups with whom I speak are often surprised to learn that Greenleaf was not in the softer pastoral or social professions, but a pragmatic businessman. They sit up and take notice when they hear of Greenleaf's long tenure at AT&T and his affiliations with prominent academic institutions like Harvard and MIT. They are impressed that his teachings are promulgated and refreshed by an international repository of Servant Leader expertise: the Greenleaf Center for Servant Leadership.

Greenleaf defines the Servant Leader as a "servant *first*. Then conscious choice brings one to aspire to lead. That person is sharply different from one who is *leader* first, perhaps because of the need to attain power or acquire material possessions." He further explains that "the difference manifests itself in the care taken by the *servant-first* to make sure that other people's highest priority needs are being served" (Greenleaf, 1970).

How is a Servant Leader recognized? Greenleaf uses the Best Test: do those served grow as persons? Do they become wiser, freer, more autonomous, more likely themselves to become servants? And what is the effect on the least privileged of society, will they benefit, or at least not be further deprived?

Over the decades, the literature has linked Servant Leadership to a broad array of positive business outcomes and organizational citizenship behaviors such as (in brief):

- Collaboration and effectiveness (Parris & Peachey, 2013)
- Service orientation (Wong & Davey, 2007)
- Helping behaviors (Erhart, 2004)
- Increased confidence in the job; perception of fairness (Walumbwa, 2010)

- Influence of/satisfaction with the supervisor (Laub, 1999)
- Innovation (Jaramillo, 2009)
- Individual and team effectiveness (Irving, 2007)
- Employee satisfaction and engagement (Cerit, 2009)
- Honest communication and trust (Hu and Liden, 2011)
- Virtuous constructs and organizational transformation (Patterson, 2003)
- Return on investment (Sipe and Frick, 2009)

These and other studies provide a foundation for Servant Leader theory and application. They help to establish a business case, a human resource case and a customer service case for Servant Leadership. For many, the "hooks" or incentives listed above are necessary to spark interest in adopting new approaches to leadership. For others, Servant Leadership research simply validates their long-held leadership instincts and convictions.

In addition to the above research, plenty of other resources are available to help understand and utilize Servant Leadership. Keith and Spears are among my favorites for explicating Greenleaf's ideas. For models, I am drawn to the "Ten Characteristics of the Servant Leader" (Spears, 2005)...

Characteristics of the Servant Leader

1. Puts people first—listening is a healing attitude
2. Uses power ethically—persuasion as preferred mode
3. Seeks consensus—compassionate collaborator
4. Practices foresight—the only lead a leader has
5. Skilled communicator—making the message real
6. Art of withdrawal—going within; replenishing
7. Acceptance—meets people where they are
8. Conceptualizes—thinks systemically
9. Nurtures community—unlimited mutual liability
10. Chooses to serve—leads with moral authority

FIGURE 5

… and the *Seven Pillars of Servant Leadership* (Sipe and Frick, (2009)…

The Seven Pillars

1. Person of Character
2. Puts People First
3. Skilled Communicator
4. Compassionate Collaborator
5. Has Foresight
6. Systems Thinker
7. Leads with Moral Authority

FIGURE 6

While these attributes will not be examined systematically here, a few that have figured prominently in VHA's experience will be featured throughout the text. Models like these and others are important tools: they provide a framework to focus thought and an exemplar toward which to strive. They also afford a jumping-off point for inquisitive and original thought.

LEADERSHIP 101

So let's back up a moment and review some leadership basics. Northouse's (1997) work in this area is coherent and useful.

- Trait Theory asserts that certain innate characteristics predispose to leadership. Here, only those born with the right qualities can be leaders.

- Process Theory has to do with the context of interactions between leaders and followers. In that case, leadership can be learned.

There is thought-provoking literature concluding that some physical and personality characteristics (gender, height, body shape, confidence and sociability) may improve one's chances of being selected for a leadership position (trait theory), whereas Servant Leadership is centered on relational interfaces that can be practiced by almost anyone (process theory).

Leaders influence others toward a common mission or goal. Sometimes that influence is wielded in the form of *transactional leadership*, where an exchange occurs between leaders and followers. This is *quid pro quo* leadership: you outperform your peers and I'll give you a bonus; vote for me and I'll reduce taxes. We use transactional leadership every day. It's a legitimate route to achieving mutual goals by meeting self-interests.

Transitional leadership may be required during periods of significant change in leaders, systems, mission or methods. This is interim leadership; it is building the airplane while flying it. The organization cannot close down to re-tool: the work must proceed despite instability and uncertainty. In large organizations this happens more frequently than one would think, since upheaval can occur in small work units almost perpetually.

Transitional leadership is an operational placeholder, but nonetheless important. It is critical when there is movement from one state to another. Special skills are required to hold the organization together during change. I once had to terminate a leader who, in the words of her colleagues, "got things done, but left a bloody wake." The person who followed her was a "senior statesman": a leader with a history of accomplishment, yet who could calm the turbulence, re-focus staff and reconstitute the team.

In another example, a department was shifting from a primarily inpatient service to an outpatient service. This reflected modern clinical thinking, but was a blow to both staff and clients. The department manager was known for his "let's do it" style, but understood the need to *let go* incrementally, phase in change and gradually regain confidence and trust. When the transition was achieved, he comfortably resumed his more normal leadership style.

Transformational leadership carries us to the next level. If we accept the premise of continuous improvement, there's always another elevation to reach. Transformational leadership motivates followers to a loftier awareness, an idealized purpose, surrendering their individual goals for the greater organizational good. A transformational workplace is typically directed by a charismatic or visionary leader, one that attracts attention and inspires people.

John F. Kennedy was often considered a transformational leader. His famous quote, "Ask not what your country can do for you; ask what you can do for your country" stirred people everywhere to step beyond their own wants and needs, to literally reach for the moon. Kennedy's personal presence and the power of his words created an era later dubbed the Camelot Years.

But as effective as a transformational organization may be, Servant Leadership can raise it to yet a higher level. Farling (1999) notes the contrasts between transformational and Servant Organizations. Transformational leaders trade on their personal charisma and propel people to help them meet the leader's agenda. These leaders often share credit for success, although that is sometimes eclipsed by their "celebrity" status. These are the leaders who become corporate legends.

What is unique to SL?

Focus on serving followers for their own good, not just the good of the organization

Self-reflection, humility, the art of withdrawal

Encouraging growth and development to reach highest potential

Concern with the success of all stakeholders

Moral Authority

FIGURE 7

Servant leaders may also be charismatic, but what stands out is their humility, authenticity and posture of *primus inter pares*: first among equals. They instill a sense of collective ownership in the organization's success. Followers don't relinquish their own self-interests, but they incorporate them into the broader interests of the organization.

Servant Leaders deflect credit, redirecting acclaim to the team. What drives the Servant Leader and the transformational leader may have entirely different origins. Whether Servant Leaders have a place in history, on the world stage, or in our own lives, they are more often considered paragons than celebrities and less likely to seek the spotlight.

In my experience, the conundrum of which is better, transformational or Servant Leadership, is a constant debate. People are prepared to duel over the distinction! And what about the other leadership models, the many angles on leadership, which all have their time and place? Must the decision of which is best be either/or?

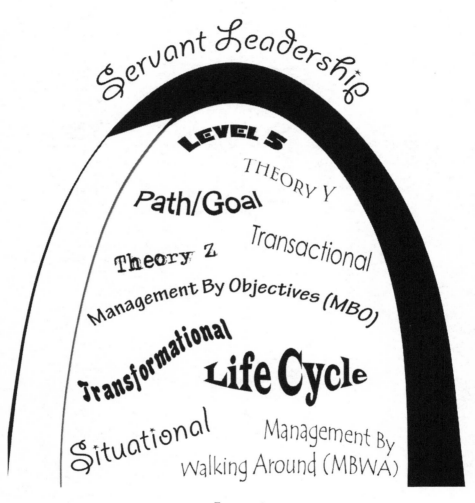

Servant Leadership

LEVEL 5

THEORY Y

Path/Goal

Transactional

Theory Z

Management By Objectives (MBO)

Transformational

Life Cycle

Situational

Management By Walking Around (MBWA)

FIGURE 8

REALITY CHECK ✓

What if I added Servant Leadership to my repertoire? For each
of the management styles above, how could Servant Leadership
enhance behavior and outcomes? Think of specific examples.

Servant Leadership is not about a single style of leading: it is a philosophy and a practice that overarches all styles of leading. It colors how we
hire and fire, plan and hold accountable, think and behave, relate and
communicate.

THE POWER PRINCIPLE

Root Cause Analysis is a method used to find the source of a problem. It
persists in asking *why, when* and *how* to peel back the layers until the core
is revealed. The premise is that only when the root cause is identified can
the problem really be solved.

And so it is with leadership. Look deeply enough and we find that
the root of leadership styles, behaviors, decisions and actions is *power*.
Our communications and interactions express the presence or absence
of power. I have long been fascinated with how we use gestures of space
(proxemics) and time (chronemics) to convey surreptitious messages of
power.

Do we keep a visitor standing or offer him a chair? Communicate
with colleagues face-to-face or email them? Sit side by side with an
employee or place a desk between us? These are examples of *proxemics*:
using spatial indicators of power.

Instances of *chronemics* can be seen when a leader continues to walk
down the hall or thumb through mail while you're talking to her, or
when you notice him checking his watch. There are sometimes legitimate
reasons to engage in these actions, but demonstration of power is not one
of them.

In hierarchical organizations, the *optic* of power is the pyramid. Someone once said, "Being on a pedestal is just another form of isolation."

And so Servant Leadership is based on upending the hierarchy, inverting the pyramid. Shown simply:

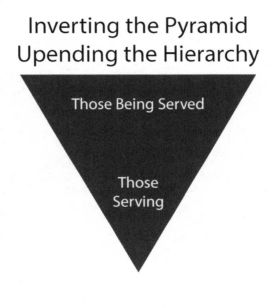

Inverting the Pyramid
Upending the Hierarchy

Those Being Served

Those
Serving

FIGURE 9

An upended pyramid is a statement of power.

For purposes of teaching Servant Leadership, I often change the labels on the inverted pyramid to Non-Supervisory/Supervisory, or Front Line/Mid-Level/Executive. I also use the Mall Map activity in Chapter 1. These exercises are important to help people at all levels to interpret Servant Leadership in their own environment, to reach past the philosophy to the daily practice of Servant Leadership.

What will each of us do differently once we are exposed to Servant Leadership? That is not a rhetorical question: it demands serious thought and commitment. What does it look like for the maintenance worker? How does a fiscal clerk apply it? How is the physician Servant Leader unique to her peers? What makes the hospital administrator stand out as a Servant Leader?

The answers are extremely personal. Although the essential principles of Servant Leadership don't vary, how each of us actualizes them can be wildly—and delightfully—individual.

A word here about the last phrase of Greenleaf's Best Test, "And what is the effect on the least privileged in society; will they benefit or at least not be further deprived?"

Define the least privileged in your milieu. Does it mean, literally, those who lack food or shelter? Can it also refer to those who are "poor in power": the lower paid worker? Those who have no voice? The patient or consumer who is at the mercy of your good will?

In a conventional organization, power rolls downhill and there is less available to whomever is at the bottom. Who is at the bottom of the hill in your situation? Upending the pyramid is a positive step in redistributing the power.

In *command and control* organizations, power is vested in positional authority. Our mental models of the military and government are cases in point (note: there are military and government entities that do practice Servant Leadership). These enterprises seek to monitor, inspect and regulate every aspect of the work: they micromanage in the vain struggle to control. They restrict power to the upper echelons, use people to their advantage, demand loyalty and are quick to place blame when mistakes are made.

The "blame game" is a slippery slope. We have all flinched at the humiliation, castigation or worse of a co-worker who made a mistake. Such treatment is a failure of leadership that reverberates across an organization, sending the clear lesson, "Don't make a mistake; if you do, don't admit it, and don't get caught!"

> *A real leader is not the top dog who merely shouts down orders. A leader is one who holds the space for the brilliance of others.*
>
> — Marianne Williamson

How often in the news do we hear one political/governmental/media agency or another calling for public dismissals or for "heads to roll"? Such actions are often calculated to show strength, but rarely lead to sensible solutions. They may meet immediate needs for retribution, but are generally uninformed and counterproductive. Beware the posturing, outrage and finger-pointing of the power model!

Control is an illusion. It's not a matter of whether crises will occur: it's a matter of when. There could never be enough safeguards to ensure a problem-free, crisis-free workplace. But an engaged, psychologically safe, servant-led workplace predisposes to fewer problems, less crisis.

In Servant Leader organizations, power is vested in moral authority and dispersed through the ranks. These leaders teach and coach; they message and model the values of the organization; they are cheerleaders for their employees. They understand that many mistakes are really systems errors and so when a mistake is made, they go on "glitch hunts, not witch hunts."[4] A service mentality extends to everyone the organization touches: customers, staff, families, providers, suppliers, contractors and the community.

Power is not a "four-letter word." *"Power over," "power for"* and *"power with"* are miles apart. The right use of power is a privilege and a responsibility of leaders. Power coupled with foresight, ethics and compassion is a world-changer. Kent Keith is on target when he says, "Realistically, someone will be in power. Servant Leaders can accumulate and exercise power, can become angry and do battle, but they do it on behalf of others."

One way Servant Leaders do this is by being "first among equals." The tenet of *primus inter pares* connotes a sharing or dispersion of power throughout the organization.

This is not done haphazardly: staff are well-trained and capable of assuming their portion of the power. It is commensurate with their ability and accretes as dependability is verified. *Primus inter pares* is not an abdication of responsibility: the leader is *always* accountable. Servant Leadership does not relieve the positional leader of answerability. This is where the buck stops.

The Servant Leader's focus is less on hierarchy and formal titles and more on empowering the team. He/she does not centralize power, but offers others a *seat at the table.* This leader ensures that authority

---

4   Thank you, Myrna Casebolt.

is stewarded ethically and that consensus is achieved where possible. Regrettably, unilateral decision-making is still the rule in many organizations, and obtaining nominal feedback is often just window-dressing.

Let's be clear about consensus: it is not "decision-making by committee" or "managing by vote." It is not waiting for all the data to come in before acting (analysis paralysis); it's not necessarily 100% agreement. Consensus indicates acceptance of a way forward, usually after give-and-take discussion. While some participants might prefer Option B, they can live with Option A, are willing to give it a try, and won't attempt to undermine it. Consensus matures in a group where trust has developed over time and where the leader is willing to fine-tune a decision or make mid-course correction if necessary.

Remember that Building Consensus is the third Characteristic of a Servant Leader. Recall also our acknowledgement that decision-making is inevitably situational. There are surely times when a leader must make an immediate decision. So how do those correspond? I like to think about consensus building more as a process than a rule: gathering input, weighing the input, making the decision and communicating transparently how I came to that decision.

Using consensus buys trust and good faith for those times when a leader must produce a speedy, unilateral decision. Consensus building is consistent with Servant Leadership. It allows a team to weigh in, pose "what ifs," offer suggestions and alternatives and consider unintended consequences. It teaches the team to participate in the thought process and share in the solution: in essence, to practice Servant Leadership themselves. It's the antithesis of a patriarchal, hierarchical system where people wait to be told what to do, then sabotage or ride out decisions they don't understand or support.

At the start of my VA career, many of my direct reports were accustomed to a command and control environment. They were more comfortable taking orders and saluting. When I began to involve them in decision-making, I developed a reputation as a "consensus leader." In honesty, that was not meant to be a compliment, but an indictment. That caused me to feel apologetic and defensive.

This is when I learned the value of labeling[5], calling to attention a point that would otherwise remain silent or assumed. In a subsequent leadership meeting, I raised an issue and asked for opinions and recommendations as to a course of action, my usual practice. I requested that any further thoughts be forwarded to me within three days. At the end of that period, I called the group together and said, "Thank you for your feedback. Considering all the possibilities, *I have decided to....*" I watched as several participants became more alert, showed renewed interest. In truth, I was not in any way changing how I made decisions: I was simply labeling the fact that I had made one! "I have decided to..." appeared to allay misgivings about consensus and reinforce my credibility as a decision-maker.

With patience and persistence, this group ultimately realized the advantage of being a "team of leaders." Now when someone calls me a consensus leader I say, "Thank you for noticing!"

Power corrupts; absolute power corrupts absolutely. Leaders can take only as much power as followers are willing to give. Servant Leaders hold power *in trust*.

As a youngster, my daughter would sing a song. "Love is something that if you give it away, you end up getting more." Power is the same; it actually increases when it is shared.

CONNECTING THE DOTS

Servant Leaders are *in connection*. According to the University of Michigan (Dutton, 2003), being in connection is humanizing and requires three qualities (elaboration added):

- *Respectful Engagement*: having honest, caring conversations with each other. The conversations we most need to have are often the hardest to initiate. That is the emphasis of VHA's CREW (Civility, Respect and Engagement in the Workplace) initiative,

---

5   Thank you, Sue Dyrenforth.

which improves workgroup satisfaction, tolerance and effective-ness. This quality also reflects the Servant Leader key compe-tency of listening. Greenleaf defined listening as a healing atti-tude. What a beautiful thought! Any of us who make the effort to really listen—reflectively, actively and compassionately—can be healers.

- *Engender Trust*: we trust that which is reliable and consistent, where words and deeds are aligned, and where truth-telling is upheld. The Servant Organization models this quality and confirms it unfailingly by its actions, even when—especially when—it is a challenge to do so.

- *Facilitate Each Other's Success*: this quality reminds me of the ninth characteristic of a Servant Leader, "nurturing community and showing unlimited mutual liability." This quality exacts more than a 50/50 effort: it asks us each to give 100%. Rather than competing with colleagues (e.g., for resources or recogni-tion), what can we do to make them shine? In a Servant Orga-nization, we bask in each other's light.

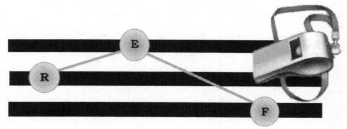

REALITY CHECK ✓

What two things will I commit to doing starting tomorrow to grow as a Servant Leader?

1._____

2._____

In the next hour, tell two people about your commitment. We are more likely to follow through on a commitment that is stated aloud.

Robert Greenleaf (2009) described the ultimate goals of Servant Leadership as:

- Creating more Servant Leaders
- Establishing a culture of Servant Leadership
- Organizations become Servant-institutions
- Servant-institutions focus on serving their employees, customers and communities
- The quality of our lives improves, and we live in a more just and caring society

OUR ROLE AS SERVANT LEADERS

Servant Leadership is not a "one and done" proposition: it's a process. We learn and grow, we take a step backward, we adapt and try again, we reach the next juncture, we grow some more. A psychologist friend who witnesses my impatience constantly reminds me to *trust the process.*[6] As part of that process, I regularly engage in an internal dialog about the kind of Servant Leader I endeavor to be:

✓ **What should I do?**

- Be *intentional* about crafting the culture. Make it what you want it to be.
- Teach, then model what you teach.

✓ **Where should I do it?**

- Fly at 30,000 feet. Withstand the pressure to live in the weeds.

---

6   Thank you, Kasey Kruer.

✓ **How should I do it?**

- Build bridges, not silos; community not competition.

- Infiltrate the organization with Servant Leaders! We're all leaders, all the time.

✓ **Why should I do it?**

- Service is not a byproduct of leadership: *it is the whole point.*

✓ **How will I know when I've done it?**

- You are not a Servant Leader until others see you as one.

The 2,000 year-old Chinese text, *Tao Te Ching*, says it this way:

 *The least desirable leader is one whom followers despise and defy; next comes the one whom they fear; better is the one whom they love and praise. But the highest leader is one of whose existence they are barely aware. The greatest success of this leader is that when the task is accomplished, people can say, "We achieved it ourselves!"*

All Things Connected...

During the span of one evening not long ago, I saw the following on television:

- Politicians wrangling about the debt ceiling and the Affordable Care Act

- A "how to" guide for wannabe millionaires

- A report on the erosion of civil liberties in a post-9/11 world

- An expose on bank lending practices in the housing market

- A retrospective on Rosa Parks

In a society that measures its strength in wealth, position, politics and military might, the real currency is power. Those vignettes on TV were all about power.

In the right hands and with the right intention, political and financial systems can craft workable solutions, can animate "liberty and justice for all," can produce a culture of excellence and compassion in our organizations and institutions, can change an economy of consumption to one of generosity, can inspire peace.

Why then, does that not happen?

Too often the flip side is dark, disturbing, dangerous and defeating:

- When authority becomes exploitive and self-serving

- When civility, humility and service have disappeared from public discourse

- When economic egoism (greed) transforms every venue into a marketplace, where prices for goods and services reflect what the market will bear instead of what they're worth, or what might elevate the human condition.

Many of us walk through our days—our lives—feeling powerless, one of the "little guys" at the effect and mercy of the power elite, whoever they might be. After all, what can one person do?

Rosa Parks was one of the little guys. She turned the system upside-down by saying NO. She did so at great risk, with courage, dignity and grace. She is remembered as much for how she did it as what she did.

Her actions bear witness that real power doesn't need to wield a weapon, brandish a budget, legislate law or dictate dogma. The essence of Rosa Parks' message is that *you and I are the power elite*. The significance of her life is the potential of one person, in universal connection, to spark momentous change. The legacy of her spirit is that justice and peace can never be an outward state until they are an inner state.

Many of those who galvanized the world weren't military leaders or corporate tycoons, were never elected to public office. In fact they were often "trouble-makers," upset the status quo, made us squirm in our comfortable existences: figures like Jesus of Nazareth, Martin Luther King, Gandhi, Mother Theresa, Nelson Mandela, Florence Nightingale, Rosa Parks—quiet revolutionaries who bravely swam against the tide of their times and whose lives changed the course of events.

At this time in our world, the gifts most needed by the human family are generosity, compassion, justice and peace. Each of us is empowered to "be the change we wish to see in the world." In the words of Margaret Mead, "One person can make a difference. Indeed it's the only thing that ever has."

Real power is the capacity generated by relationships. We can choose not to be shaped by the whims and wishes of the forces around us, but instead leave our mark on the world.

Peace and power always have been, always will be, "inside jobs."

...All Things Connected

TOOLBOX ACTIVITY:

Power vs Service

Do you remember the book (or movie) *One Flew Over the Cuckoo's Nest* (Kesey, 1963)? At its heart, it was a story about power and control. Servant Leaders credit every player in the organization as an important part of the team and serve them through teaching, nurturing, listening and encouraging. A Servant mindset is best demonstrated by service-oriented behaviors such as sharing power and control, creating a safe environment for honest discussions and putting others' needs first.

But good intentions can sometimes be overshadowed by external demands such as limited time and resources or the pressures of the day. A service orientation can revert to a power orientation over time. Being mindful of our own thoughts, values and behaviors is important to keep us from slipping into the traps of power and control.

∂ Instructions ∽

View any/all of these YouTube videos:
- "One Flew Over the Cuckoo's Nest - ballgame.mov"
- "Nest 1. Vote"
- "Chief Voted scene"

Note: use wording above for online search

Throughout the clip, imagine that you are a member of Nurse Ratched's therapy group. Be mindful of your own feelings and thoughts regarding Nurse Ratched.

❧ Discussion ❧

In a small group, consider the following:

- As a "participant" of the therapy session, how did you feel about the group experience? About Nurse Ratched?

- What three words would you associate with Nurse Ratched?

- Did your feelings change throughout the clip? How?

- What verbal and non-verbal behaviors made you feel that way?

- Who was the real leader in the group?

- Understanding that in a therapy session boundaries need to be maintained, could Nurse Ratched have handled this differently? What would you have done?

- What is Nurse Ratched's philosophy of power versus service?

- Do you believe she became a nurse with this philosophy? Or did it evolve?

- How could that have happened?

- Can it happen to us?

- What about the nurse who was Nurse Ratched's assistant: what stands out about her behavior and why do you suspect that is so?

- When did you last display a power orientation? From your insights about Nurse Ratched, what can you do to replace your own power-oriented behaviors with service-oriented behaviors?

- What specifically can we do to ensure we maintain a service orientation?

Servant Leadership is not a technique, but a way of life. It is important to be patient with yourself as you continue to grow and challenge yourself as a Servant Leader. What might seem like a small behavioral change may leave an indelible impression on those around you.

Chapter References

Cerit, Y. (2009). "The effects of Servant Leader behaviors of school principals on teachers' job satisfaction." Educational Management Administration and Leadership, 37 (5), 600-623.

Chand, S. (2015). "William Ouchi's Theory Z of Motivation." www. articlelibrary.com/motivation/william-ouchis-theory-z-of-motivation

Collins, J. (2001). *Good to Great*. New York: Harper Business.

Drucker, P. (1954). *The Practice of Management*. New York: Harper Business.

Dutton, J. E. (2003). *Energize Your Workplace: How to Create and Sustain High-Quality Connections at Work*. San Francisco, CA: Jossey-Bass.

Erhart, M. G. (2004). "Leadership and Procedural Justice Climate as Antecedents of Unit Level Organizational Citizenship Behaviors." Personnel Psychology, 57, 61-94.

Farling, M. L., Stone, A. G. and Winston, B. E. (1999). *Servant Leadership: Setting the Stage for Empirical Research*. Journal of Leadership Studies, 6, 49-62.

Greenleaf, R. K. (1970). *The Servant as Leader*. Atlanta, GA: The Greenleaf Center for Servant Leadership.

Greenleaf, R. K. (2009). *The Institution as Servant*. Westfield, IN: The Greenleaf Center for Servant Leadership.

Greenleaf, R. K. (2013). *Servant: Retrospect and Prospect*. Westfield, IN: Greenleaf Center for Servant Leadership.

Hersey, P. and Blanchard, K. H. (1969). "Life Cycle Theory of Leadership." Training and Development Journal, Vol. 23 (5), 26-34.

House, R. J. (Sep. 1971). "A Path Goal Theory of Leadership Effectiveness." Administrative Science Quarterly, Vol. 16, No 3, 321-339.

Hu, J. and Liden, R.C. (2011). "Antecedents of team potency and team effectiveness: An examination of goal and process clarity and servant leadership." Journal of Applied Psychology, 1-12.

Irving, J. A. and Longbotham, G. J. (2007). "Team effectiveness and six essential themes: a Regression model based on items in the organizational leadership assessment. International Journal of Leadership Studies, 2 (2), 98-113.

Jaramillo, F., Grisaffe, D. B., Chonko, L. B. and Roberts, J. A. (2009b). "Examining the impact of Servant Leadership on salesperson's turnover intention." Journal of Personal Selling and Sales Management, 29 (4), 351-365.

Keith, K. M. (2008.) *The Case for Servant Leadership*. Westfield IN: Greenleaf Center for Servant Leadership.

Keith, K. M. (2013). "Growing to Greatness through Servant Leadership." www.toservefirst.com/...Growing to Greatness%20 through-Servant-Leadership

Kesey, K. (1963). *One Flew Over the Cuckoo's Nest*. New York: Signet.

Lao Tzu. *Tao Te Ching*. Verse 17. Acc6.its.brooklyn.cuny.edu/~phalsall/texts/taote

Laub, J. A. (1999). "Assessing the servant organization: Development of the servant organization leadership assessment instrument." Dissertation Abstracts International, 60, (02), 308.

MacGregor, D. (1960). *The Human Side of Enterprise*. New York: McGraw-Hill.

Mead, M. www.brainyquotes.com

Northouse, P. G. (1997). *Leadership: Theory and Practice*. USA: Sage Publications.

Parris, D. L. and Peachey, J. W. (2013). "A systemic literature review of Servant Leadership Theory in Organizational Contexts." Journal of Business Ethics, 113, 377-393.

Patterson, K. (2003). "Servant Leadership: A Theoretical Model." Dissertation Abstracts, International, 64 (2), 570.

Sipe, J. W. and Frick, D. M. (2015). *Seven Pillars of Servant Leadership*. New York/New Jersey: Paulist Press.

Spears, L. (2005). O*n Character and Servant Leadership: Ten characteristics of effective, caring leaders*. Westfield, IN: Greenleaf Center for Servant Leadership.

Walumbwa, F. O. (2010). "Servant leadership, procedural justice climate, service climate and organizational citizenship behavior: a Cross-level investigation." Journal of Applied Psychology, 95, (3), 517-529.

Williamson, M. www.AZQuotes.com

Wong, P. T. P. and Davey, D. (2007). "Best Practices in Servant Leadership." Paper presented at the Servant Leadership Research Roundtable, Regent University, Virginia Beach, VA.

CHAPTER FOUR

*Servant Leadership in Veterans
Health Administration*

All Things Connected...

I AM A VETERAN

I served my country.
I left the people I loved,
And learned to kill without flinching.
I was dusted with Agent Orange,
I froze and I sweltered.
I wept freely over letters from home,
Unable to shed a tear for the body at my feet.
And when I couldn't change reality,
I found ways to alter my mental landscape.
I left my leg there, and my best friend,
And part of my soul.
I saw and felt terror
Of which I cannot speak,
And I will not allow myself to think.
I fought proudly for my country,
Yet sometimes I feel it betrayed me.
I am still in pain.
Fear and anger are but a blink away.
Sometimes my spirit hurts
Even more than my body.
I don't want to live in the past,
But please remember this:
When I come to you for something
To ease whatever my affliction;
When I seem the most demanding;
When I complain the loudest
And resist the hardest,
What I am really seeking is *connection*.

I AM NOT A VETERAN

But I serve my country
By taking care of those who were.
What I know of war
I learned in high school.
I am detached from battle—and from you—
By time and perception.
But I hear the stories you tell
When you risk telling them,
Or when I risk listening.
Still it's all too easy to forget or ignore,
When you're back for the third time in a week,
Looking for some relief (or absolution)
That I cannot give you;
When I begin to see you as an obstacle to my
     work,
Instead of the very reason for it;
When there are twenty more in line behind you
And the resources don't stretch that far,
And the clock is ticking,
And I can't help you,
And you won't help me try.
But please remember this:
When I appear frustrated or frenetic,
When I judge you by the standards of my life
And not the realities of your own;
When I protect my mental landscape
By preserving the distances between us;
What I am really seeking is *connection*.

When Johnny Comes Marching Home Again ...
—Civil War Song

OVERVIEW OF VA

The mission of the Department of Veterans Affairs (VA) is to fulfill President Lincoln's promise *"to care for him who shall have borne the battle..."* by serving the men and women who are America's Veterans. Honoring that promise to the more than 22 million Veterans living today, and by extension to their families, is an awesome responsibility. It is a task that requires a massive organization capable of touching Veterans over a lifetime.

VA is structured into three business lines or Administrations:

- The National Cemetery Administration (NCA), which handles memorials and burials at sites across the country

- The Veterans Benefits Administration (VBA), which provides compensation and pensions, education through the GI Bill, home mortgages, employment services and vocational rehabilitation

- The Veterans Health Administration (VHA), which delivers comprehensive health care, including primary and specialty

care, mental health and long-term care, prosthetics and rehabilitation. VHA also plays a major role in the education of
physicians, nurses and many other clinical professionals, is a
leader in medical research and provides support in national
emergencies

VHA is by far the largest segment of VA. Its physical footprint
includes more than 1,500 sites of care, including Medical Centers, community based outpatient clinics, residential rehab centers and community living centers (nursing homes). In 1996, VHA began a seismic shift
from a *hospital system* to a *health care system*, bringing care not just to the
bedside, but to wherever the Veteran is.

VHA is one of the largest health care employers in the world and
the nation's largest integrated health care system. VHA serves over 9 million enrolled Veterans through a workforce of more than 300 thousand
health care professionals and support staff, many of whom are Veterans
themselves.

Most people are unaware of VHA's many "claims to fame." VHA
has been a leader in technology (e.g., electronic medical records, bar-
coded medication administration, and telehealth capabilities), quality
and health outcomes (e.g., national customer service indices and health
quality indicators), spinal cord injury and prosthetics innovations and
countless others. Several years ago, VHA was touted as the "best care
anywhere" in a book by the same name (Longman, 2012).

So let's address the elephant in the room. As a federal agency, VA is
often in the spotlight. More attention is paid to sensational news stories
about VA's problems than its accomplishments. I am not an apologist for
VA, but the truth is that VA's issues are often politicized and critics are
not always well-informed. The truth is that like all health care systems,
VA makes mistakes and has failures. But VA sets the standard in owning
up to them, learning from them and then raising the bar. The truth is that
most VA employees deliver exceptional care and service, and they do it
with integrity and compassion. And yet the truth is that if VA has failed
even one Veteran, it's not good enough.

It was amidst a flurry of negative press that I was scheduled to make a series of significant national presentations. How distinctly uncomfortable! Halfway through my speech, a hand was raised in the audience and the participant challenged how I could credibly relate VA and Servant Leadership. "They are miles apart," he said. I immediately recalled a family member who, when asked why he did not attend church replied, "Because the people sitting in the pews on Sunday are the same ones out there sinning the rest of the week!"

So, I would think, who needs church more than sinners? Instead of looking at those people as hypocrites, I saw them as individuals who struggled and sometimes failed, but who regularly sought inspiration and sustenance to become their best selves. Organizations are like that, too. Who needs Servant Leadership more than organizations who are struggling to serve at their highest level? VA reflects the overwhelming majority of workplaces who have not yet attained the mountaintop, who are *works in progress.*

Continuous Quality Improvement is the concept in health care that we can always do better, there is always another level of excellence to be achieved. New knowledge, new technology and new skills intersect with higher professional standards and higher patient expectations. To meet that challenge, VA embarked on a course of transformation.

VA'S TRANSFORMATIONAL AGENDA

The heart of the effort and its jumping off point was a resolution to adopt a Patient Centered Care philosophy. That may sound intuitive for a health care organization, but it's not. Hospitals become "institutional" over time. They can run on rules, not relationships, schedule care for the hospital's convenience, instead of the patient's. Buildings may be difficult to navigate and the jargon hard to understand. The environment is traditionally sterile and uninviting, food might be unfamiliar and unappetizing. Families can get lost in the urgency of events.

Patient Centered Care puts things back into proper perspective. Patients and families become partners in their care. Environments are welcoming and user-friendly. Scheduling revolves around the patient's availability, and care options include group visits, telehealth and phone appointments. Test results and health promotion materials are posted on confidential patient portals. Some patients are assigned health coaches to help meet their personal wellness goals. Integrative modalities like acupuncture and meditation are available.

Remember the graphic in Figure 4?

Transformational Workplace

Patient Centered Care, Customer Service
Safe, Timely, Quality Outcomes

Serving the Veteran

Veteran-Centric

Serving the Employee

CREW (Civility)
Systems Redesign
Effective Teams

Employee Engagement

Leadership

Serving the Organization

Integrated Ethics
Learning Organization
Servant Leadership

At this point in the transformation, the organization was fast-tracking a metamorphosis in the Veteran/patient centered sphere and had cultivated invested and empowered employees to accomplish that. Transformation was occurring in models of care and in relationships.

To reap the greatest benefit of all this effort, however, it was critical that an *intentional culture of leadership* be espoused and replicated at all levels of management and supervision. It had to be a cultural model that unleashed the potential of all staff, provided a platform for engaged employees and teams to give patient centered care within an attitude of service, and that upheld an organizationally healthy way of doing business.

It was apparent that Servant Leadership was the ideal framework for the transformation VA desired. Given the compelling forces buffeting

health care today, VA and Servant Leadership seem to be natural partners. External pressures like legislation, Congressional oversight, public
expectations and the demands of consumerism, and internal stressors like
diminishing resources, workforce barriers, and rigorous benchmarks of
quality, accessible and timely care conspire to exert a push-pull dynamic.

FIGURE 10

Servant Leadership brings about a moderating influence to those
pressures by maintaining a holistic and contextual perspective. It helps:

- Maximize human assets
- Optimize budget dollars and create value
- Improve quality and outcomes
- Manage constant, unpredictable change
- Ensure a positive experience for Veteran patients and their
  families
- Develop leaders with courage and vision
- Support a transformational environment

Servant Leadership serves VA's transformational agenda by linking the organization's top priorities:

- Personalized, proactive, Veteran-centered care
- Civil, engaged workforce
- High-performing teams
- Customer service
- Results-driven
- Ethics
- Learning organization
- Diversity & inclusion
- Systems redesign
- Managing change
- Psychological safety
- Succession planning

FIGURE 11

It also aligns seamlessly with VA's **I CARE** values (integrity, commitment, advocacy, respect and excellence) and VA leadership competencies (leading people, leading change, business acumen, results-driven, building coalitions and global perspective.) All things really are connected!

Implementing Servant Leadership in VHA was far from easy: there were many challenges to change. Most obvious was the sheer size of the organization. How do you educate a cadre of 22 thousand positional leaders? The entire workforce? In a consistent way? Across a national stage? The practicalities and logistics of such an endeavor were overwhelming.

System-wide change of any kind is formidable enough in private sector companies, where flexibility and agility are assumed, and leaders and the Board of Directors are in alignment. A bureaucratic organization nested in a political environment is another story. "Red tape" is a reality of government, where layers of approval, labor negotiations, feedback from multiple (and often conflicting) stakeholder groups consume time and political capital, where the Board of Directors is the Congress of the United States.

Underlying the obstacles of size and bureaucracy are the realities of culture change. As discussed in Chapter Two, culture change takes time to become embedded in the organization. In a political environment, time is often measured by the term of office. With the revolving-door leadership of elected or appointed officials, there is a rush to commence and complete a change process during the leader's tenure. That process may be discarded or reversed when a new leader is appointed and yet another project initiated. Since culture is built on behaviors and habits, there may not be time enough for the culture change to "stick."

REALITY CHECK ✓

List a few of the obstacles to & accelerators of change
in your organization.

OBSTACLES   ACCELERATORS

What will it take to move them from the left column
to the right column? How can you begin to do
that? Whose help will you need to enlist?

As in most institutions, there were accelerating factors that spurred VA on:

- The changing context of health care
- Congruence with enterprise priorities
- Alignment with values and core competencies

Perhaps the best catalyst for Servant Leadership in VHA was the mounting sense that a new leadership model was essential, that the methods of the past were not sufficient to pass the tests of the future. A groundswell of interest, the growing community of "converts" and a deliberative garnering of corporate support really made this a propitious moment in time.

There were also obstacles that hindered VA's progress:

- The size of the system
- Government/political environment
- Revolving-door leadership
- Realities of culture change
- Common misperceptions

COMMON MISPERCEPTIONS

As efforts unfolded to teach VA leaders across the system, I encountered a stubbornly prevalent roadblock: a common misunderstanding about what Servant Leadership is and what it is not. Questions, reservations and misinformed beliefs about Servant Leadership were so frequent and so similar that I soon incorporated frank discussion of them up front, instead of waiting for the predictable questions to arise. Those misperceptions fell into four categories that invited closer inspection and response.

How I identified and addressed them to VA audiences may be useful to other groups as well:

Servant Leadership isn't strong leadership. My employees would run rough-shod over me. I can't afford to be seen as a pushover.

The person who raises this point is revealing his own unhappy experience. What a sad commentary! Our culture has drawn a profile of the successful leader as a Type A personality, authoritarian, bottom-line driven, exploitive: the power model versus the service model. I recall one of my bosses who took no prisoners and showed no mercy. Meeting a deadline or beating the competition was more important than the quality of the effort. He was arrogant, intimidating and single-minded, all in the name of tough management. If this is the "face" of leadership in your world, no wonder the misperception.

Servant Leadership is not for the fainthearted! It is not soft, laissez faire or lenient. It is not an abdication of responsibility. It is not anemic leadership: it requires *strength of self-mastery, strength of action and strength of relationships.* Servant Leaders operate from courage, integrity, persistence, resilience, accountability and a steady internal compass. Servant Leaders combine humility with determination. They are resolute in where they're going, firm in how they'll get there and generous in sharing the road.

The term "servant" is a turn-off; it offends me. How can I be subservient and be an effective leader?

This question generally comes from two sources. My African-American colleagues express concern about having overcome a heritage of slavery, only to be told they must now be servants. As one co-worker put it, "I

believe in the idea of Servant Leadership, but I shiver at the terminology."
Consciously or unconsciously, emotion runs deep.

The second source is colleagues who have "come up through the ranks." Secretaries, clerks, technicians, nurses and others who have ascended the pyramid step by step, who remember clearly being "under someone's thumb," sometimes worry that Servant Leadership is a step backward.

There is a difference between service and servitude.
Servitude is coerced; service is a choice. Servitude is an inability to determine one's own course; service is a deliberate decision to serve. Choosing service is powerful. And we don't choose it once, we choose it with every decision, action and relationship. I believe that those who have known historical servitude or modest professional beginnings may, out of their own experiences, become the best Servant Leaders.

Humility is one of the distinguishing traits of a Servant Leader: a "discreet mark of perfect lucidity and unwavering standards" (Comte-Sponville, 1996). This leader is not timid or self-effacing, but unpretentious and authentic. It shows great humility on the part of the leader to allow others to lead, to help them grow in leadership. While humility may be quiet, it is not weak. It takes courage and equanimity to comfortably wear that label. It is a stamp of humility to accept the designation of *Servant*.

Some organizations amend the term Servant Leader to be more acceptable to their employees or to emphasize the characteristic: serving leadership or service leadership, for example. Others use entirely different terms but retain the philosophy and principles. The bottom line is, call it what resonates in your organization, call it what people will "hear" without hesitation. Just let the meaning be clear. The appellation is not as important as the substance.

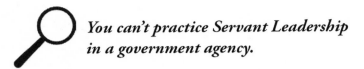

You can't practice Servant Leadership in a government agency.

For some, this reservation stems from a misapprehension that Servant Leadership is a religious concept. It is true that we find notions of service and servanthood in major world religions. We can surmise that Greenleaf's Quaker roots might have influenced his thinking about a better way to lead. But his use of Servant Leadership in a competitive business climate confirmed the value of his teaching outside the realm of religion. (For deeper discussion of this theme, see Chapter 7.) The fact is that, while Servant Leadership is not tacitly religious, it is congruent with many religious teachings. For those so inclined, it also reflects the best aspects of secular humanism.

Aside from the above, what is it about government that would seem antithetical to Servant Leadership? Is it the size and complexity? Is it the plodding pace of change? Do those outside the bureaucracy see government employees as impersonal and officious? Do those inside the bureaucracy view it as unrealistic or hopeless?

Working in a government agency is an act of stewardship. The point should not be that we *can't* practice Servant Leadership there, it's that we *had better* practice it there. The players in political and government environments, by the very nature of the game, are at peril of falling to the extremes: abuse of power on one end of the spectrum, indifference on the other. Constituents who seek help from government when they feel victimized, vulnerable and helpless are not served by either extreme. Servant Leaders can secure the middle ground, preserve the "sweet spot." They can serve with competence, compassion and grace.

Government employees used to be known as civil or public *servants.* They have *always* been servants of the people. The good news is that many Federal, State and Local government agencies around the country have been quietly practicing Servant Leadership for years, and many more are finding Servant Leadership now, clamoring for information and assistance to help them create the culture.

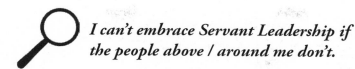 *I can't embrace Servant Leadership if the people above / around me don't.*

This is the universal plaint. Whether I am speaking about civility, Patient Centered Care, or Servant Leadership, I am constantly asked how employees can possibly practice _____ (fill in the blank), if their managers don't "get it." These questioners do "get it": they grasp the ideology and the behaviors. They see the value and they see the connections. They may practice Servant Leadership at home or in the community, but are reluctant to bring it to work in the absence of supervisory support. Servant Leadership is countercultural; Servant Leaders are revolutionaries. So there is risk. But if we wait until everyone in the management layers above us "get it," nothing will change.

Do not just assume that leaders don't subscribe to Servant Leadership. They may be as reticent as the staff reporting to them about taking the risk. Perhaps they are saying the same thing about the manager on the next rung of the ladder that you are thinking about them. I've often pictured it like this:

The Cookie Quandary

1. We're all leaders, all the time
2. We're always the cream filling in the middle

FIGURE 12

A first line supervisor, for example, is pressured by the managers above her and by the staff below her. She is expected to support management and advocate for her direct reports. She is continually interpreting, mediating and juggling demands on all sides. She can't wait to be promoted so she can leave those pressures behind.

But later as a department chief and then as an executive, she finds that nothing has changed. The names and faces may be different, but she is still being squeezed from all directions. No matter where we are on the career ladder, we are always the cream filling in the middle!

Don't write off your supervisors. Instead of presuming they're not interested in Servant Leadership, have a conversation about it, share your knowledge and passion, enlist their cooperation, build an alliance. But if your best efforts still don't meet with success…

Don't wait for the memo!

Ideally, culture change should be driven from the top; practically, it is a top-down, bottom-up, side-to-side proposition. We're all given the opportunity to lead. Each of us has a sphere of influence. There may be 300 people in your sphere of influence, or 30, or 3. You may supervise them or work alongside them. Servant Leaders are not always in positions of power, but they are always powerful people. Don't underestimate your own power to change the workplace.

GENERATING INTEREST

When I was 13 years old, I wrote a novel, *The Mystery of Dead Man's Island*. Maybe you've heard of it…or maybe not! This was long before the computer; the manuscript was pen and paper. I had no idea how to go about getting published, so I decided that if I generated enough interest in the book, some publisher would seek me out. I gathered a small group of friends; we split up and began making the rounds of bookstores and department stores. We would ask the clerk if *The Mystery of Dead Man's Island* was in stock. We would recommend the book to other customers. We even persuaded some store managers to contact their suppliers. We created the demand!

That was my first (though unsuccessful) foray into marketing. But when people started inquiring about VHA's marketing strategy for Servant Leadership, this story became my inspiration.

I had been injecting the topic into Organizational Health presentations for a while when I heard VA's highest-ranking executive mention Servant Leadership in a speech. I took that as an imprimatur to move forward. There was never any mandate from the top; I simply stepped up my game and set my sights on campaigning for Servant Leadership across the system. Partnering with a small group of colleagues, *we created the demand.*

REALITY CHECK ✓

What three actions could you take right now to "market" Servant Leadership in your organization?

1.

2.

3.

ORCHESTRATING SERVANT LEADERSHIP IN VA

With the sponsorship and support of VHA's National Center for Organization Development (NCOD), a small cohort of like-minded staff was given the autonomy to go forward. There was no proclamation: we surreptitiously, unobtrusively, purposefully and relentlessly sowed the seeds.

Raising awareness was job one. In a concerted effort to spread the word, we sought out any appropriate venue. VHA's *Organizational Health Newsletter* became a conduit of Servant Leader articles and tools. Numerous conferences are held in VHA and we managed to be included on the programs of many of them. We spoke at Senior Leadership conferences, Human Resource conferences, Mental Health conferences, Pharmacy conferences and Nursing conferences. We gave keynote addresses, break-out sessions, skill building classes and retreats.

> Servant Leadership is both a philosophy and a set of practices. Servant Leaders are persons of integrity who lead an organization to success by putting the needs of Veteran customers, employees and communities first; sharing knowledge and power; and helping people develop and perform to their highest capacity.
>
> —VHA's definition of Servant Leadership

Those events resonated with participants of all ranks and disciplines. We found that people were hungry to learn more, and we began receiving requests to customize Servant Leader training to offices, programs and at Medical Centers. Our exposure increased exponentially. We might, for example, work with a 20-person logistics department in Washington, DC one week, and a staff of hundreds at a hospital in California the next. Some were discipline-specific intensives and others covered Servant Leader basics in multi-disciplinary groups—everyone from housekeeping to physicians to administrators. By this time, we were averaging 30 presentations per year, all by invitation of senior leaders.

We reached a milestone when we were asked to instruct groups of developing or prospective leaders in Servant Leadership. These elite programs are offered by both the Department (VA) and the Administration (VHA). They are limited: applicants compete for finite slots and consent to a rigorous course of training, coaching and mentoring over a year or more, while still fulfilling their regular duties. Candidates for VA's leadership preparation are high-potential employees who are fast-tracked into the leadership pipeline.

These are VA's leaders of the future and so they are *exactly* the audience for Servant Leadership. The time to stimulate interest, develop habits and test out new behaviors is *before* assuming key leadership responsibilities. It is a joy to watch talented students learn why a Servant Leader approach is important, the "how-to's" and key practices, the results that can accrue, that it is not just acceptable in their organization, but expected. Teaching

Servant Leadership to budding leaders is an unambiguous message of executive commitment.

While elevating the consciousness inside VHA, it was also important to begin building a reputation as a Servant Leader organization. Keynote addresses were delivered at other governmental agencies and at Greenleaf conferences in the United States and Singapore. VA was extended a seat on the Board of Trustees of the Greenleaf Center, where I was honored to serve. This association with the Greenleaf Center grew to be a mutually beneficial relationship, helping VA to deepen its commitment.

My job demanded a great deal of travel, and I was delighted to see evidence of Servant Leadership in field-based VA facilities wherever I went. I found hidden gems: hospital Directors who had been Servant Leaders for years, an innovative educational partnership between Viterbo University[7] and a Wisconsin VA Medical Center, inclusion of Servant Leadership language in VISN succession planning and strategic planning documents, local performance-based interview questions and performance goals crafted around Servant Leadership principles. While it was gratifying that Servant Leadership was seeping into the "real work" of VA health care, it was frustrating that "corporate VA" was not setting the pace, but playing catch-up with what was occurring in the field!

As an organization, we were now well into the journey, but how far had we come and how far was there to go? We needed to find a way to measure our progress, one employee at a time.

THE SERVANT LEADER 360

A 360 degree assessment tool is like a telescope that follows the orbit of an employee in his workplace. It goes beyond the typical boss/worker evaluation. The individual completes a self-assessment and asks supervisors, peers and subordinates to rate him as well. That circumferential view is illuminating. It gives us a glimpse into how people regard us from every

---

7   Thank you, Tom Thibodeau.

angle. Three hundred and sixty degree assessments are widely used in a variety of organizations. NCOD already administered one that measured VA's leadership competencies. But while there are clear correlations, there are nuances in Servant Leadership competencies that are not captured in the VA or other organizations' tools.

To remedy that, it was decided to either locate or develop a tool that would meet the following criteria:

- Based on a guiding model with an accompanying text

- Behaviorally grounded

- Provided actionable information

- Consistent with VA's culture and vernacular

IDENTIFYING THE MODEL

To begin, we reviewed 13 of the most referenced and most recently published models of Servant Leadership. Five of those had associated assessments. *The Seven Pillars of Servant Leadership* by James Sipe and Don Frick (2009) seemed to be the best fit and needed the least amount of adaptation to meet the criteria. (The abridged version of our process follows. For a comprehensive scholarly treatment of VHA's SL360, consult McCarren, Lewis-Smith, Belton, et al., 2016.)

With the Seven Pillars as our guiding model, we conducted an extensive literature review, searching for existing Servant Leadership assessments. None sufficiently suited the criteria or reflected the guiding model, so we set out to create our own. Starting with 246 publically available assessment questions, independent raters sorted each item for fit with our criteria and reduced the number of items. They were further winnowed by a team knowledgeable in Servant Leadership. Where necessary, items were modified or new items constructed altogether in order to form a coherent *gestalt* of the Seven Pillars.

The initial survey went through several rounds of evaluation: first by a larger group of staff who were not versed in Servant Leadership, to assess coherence with the model and basic comprehension of the tool. Eliminations and modifications were made as a result. The subsequent draft was reviewed by external subject matter experts whose feedback was used to strengthen the remaining items and sub-competencies. After each round of review, research professionals from NCOD exercised the necessary scientific and technical rigor to ensure the final product would be reliable and valid. The ultimate assessment comprised 61 items, 93% of which were original or significantly revised. (See the narrative version of the SL 360 in its entirety at the end of this chapter: Figure 14.)

The VHA SL 360[8], as it was fondly christened, was a behaviorally based, action-oriented assessment tool built on Servant Leader competencies. It was made available to VA leaders in late 2013. The SL 360 is an electronic tool administered through NCOD at regular intervals. A coordinator provides an orientation to the instrument and monitors the process. Participants receive an automated report consisting of:

- Their average scores by type of respondent
- An Interpretation Guide
- General information about Servant Leadership
- A comprehensive Development Guide for personal action planning, including:
    o Tools, tips and templates
    o A list of additional resources
- An optional individual coaching session

As of this writing, more than ten thousand participants and respondents have accessed the SL 360.

8   Thank you, Heather McCarren, Jamie Smith, Jaimee Robinson and Boris Yanovsky.

SETTING THE COURSE

VA now had a suite of materials to facilitate the spread of Servant Leadership: a plethora of education and training options, newsletters and communication tools and a unique mechanism to measure and motivate growth. But all that material and data are of little benefit if it sits on a shelf. The nuts and bolts of Servant Leadership is the challenging part, and so we synthesized some strategies to help leaders map out their course. Through an average of 60 requests for consultation per year, NCOD "companioned" leaders and leadership teams on their journey. This patient attention and support was an important factor in helping them translate information into action. The following guidance developed for VA leaders can be useful as well to anyone striving to "fast forward" as a Servant Leader.

WHAT TO DO WITH THE INFORMATION?

Establishing a baseline is a good first step and a 360 degree assessment meets that need. But what if you don't have access to such a tool? How can one gain self-awareness? A "Living 360," the face-to-face equivalent of an electronic or paper survey, is one option. Using a person who is trusted and skilled at interviewing, some of the same questions can be put to bosses, colleagues and direct reports, with even richer results.

If that is not a viable alternative, you can ask selected co-workers yourself. Let them know you are working on becoming a Servant Leader and that you value their feedback. If the work environment is psychologically safe, you'll be surprised at how obliging many people will be. By simply asking, you're conveying the message that you're serious; you are exemplifying Servant Leader behavior.

Using the Seven Pillars as a framework helps many to understand where their improvement efforts will best pay off. Think about creating a Personal Development Plan around the Pillars. Most of us zoom in on our weakest areas, but it's important to be aware of our strengths as well as opportunities for improvement. Don't allow the areas you have already mastered to backslide while you work on correcting others. Since you can't concentrate on all elements at once, prioritize what areas may have the biggest impact or facilitate your improvement in other Pillars.

Consider how ratings may vary by category of respondent: i.e., did you select respondents who were likely to give you honest feedback, or those who would only give you positive comments? Are some groups' ratings significantly higher or lower than others? If so, can you determine a functional explanation for that (does it reflect the nature of your work with this group)? Do your direct reports evaluate you differently than your bosses or peers? Are there gaps between how others rate you and how you assess yourself?

Feedback is a gift! Don't fall into the trap of rationalizing or discounting less than stellar feedback; use it to discern how you can grow as a Servant Leader. Identify several resources you will consult, specific actions you will take, and commit to reassessing your progress at a later date. The Personal Development Plan template in Figure 15 at the end of this chapter may help you get started.

IS SERVANT LEADERSHIP RIGHT FOR YOU?

FIGURE 13

The way forward is not always smooth! As leaders introduce Servant Leadership into their workplace, they may expect to encounter both enthusiasm and resistance.

Some staff will be early adopters: these are your "champions." Others are unsure of where this will lead and what will be expected of them, but they are tantalized and willing to keep an open mind. From a few, there may be active resistance. Don't shut it down! This is a fear response: *What does it mean? How will things change? How will I need to change? I understand/am comfortable with the old way of doing things.*

Some will get on board when they see others acclimate and gain confidence. Others will store it away, but discover it again as their leadership matures. A few may never find Servant Leadership compatible and choose to leave the organization. Those who find Servant Leadership an "over my dead body" proposition do themselves and the organization a great favor by acknowledging the fact and moving to better-suited terrain. Servant Leadership cannot be mandated: it is always a choice. *Trust the process.*

BUILDING AND SUPPORTING THE CULTURE

The goal is to build a culture of Servant Leadership. In the best case, that begins with the executive team, gathers momentum through the supervisory ranks and flows throughout the organization. There is no playbook: only guiding principles. It would be so much easier to circulate a checklist—check, check, check, done! But each employee must translate principles into practice. How can each person demonstrate Servant Leadership wherever they are?

As stated earlier, leaders must use consistent messaging and modeling to craft the culture. The immediate supervisor may be the most influential model for her staff. Talking about Servant Leadership while acting in a way that denies it will quickly kill the effort.

Every organization, and each workgroup in an organization, has a reputation. Some are known for their customer service or their technical expertise. Others are characterized as "closed" or hard to deal with. What is the *trademark* of your workgroup? How do you want it to be known? What characteristics and behaviors will define your corporate identity? A culture of Servant Leadership won't just materialize: it requires a plan that is thoughtful and intentional. Leaders can prompt specific actions to anchor the direction and trigger opportunities to reaffirm it. How can you "brand" your workplace as a Servant Leader organization?

If kicking off the culture is challenging, sustaining it can be formidable. The initial "rah-rah" has dwindled and the hard work of *enculturation* proceeds. So again a plan is vital. This may take the form of regular activities like book/article discussions and "lunch and learn" events, special occurrences such as Servant Leader "refresh" days and outside speakers, supportive practices including regular opportunities for individual or collective reflection and "encouragement groups."

Encouragement groups are small clusters of leader peers or colleagues who meet to bolster their Servant Leader practices. VA Medical Centers which have embraced this technique have formulated some guidelines:

- The group should not be led by the top executive, although it must be clear that there is executive sponsorship

- The group should be assured time to meet on a regular basis, and also when there is an *ad hoc* need

- There should be a focus. This is not a time to vent, but to discuss real-time challenges to being a Servant Leader. Venting is fine for a moment, but then the group needs to move on

- The group provides support for each other; companionship on the journey

- Some groups develop a framework for communicating to staff: how to label Servant Leader behaviors they are exhibiting and how/when to acknowledge examples of Servant Leader behavior they observe in staff

- The group sets a tone and models Servant Leader behavior in its daily work

- They compassionately share their failures in Servant Leadership and help by suggesting different approaches, in a safe environment

- They congratulate each other on their successes

The sustainment plan should incorporate systematic Servant Leader communication through meetings, Town Halls and newsletters, echoing the message at every possible occasion. Using the techniques of *linking and labeling* can be particularly effective. *Labeling* Servant Leader behaviors when they are observed is a source of public recognition and a visible affirmation of the conduct we want to perpetuate. *Linking* Servant Leadership to organizational priorities and goals helps to connect them in people's minds as "not just one more thing to do, but the way we do everything."

Any plan must account for turnover. How will the group integrate newcomers who may never have heard of Servant Leadership? And what happens if the leader/leaders who led the culture change retire or leave the organization? What if the new leader does not endorse Servant Leadership? These questions emphasize the imperative of a sustainment plan. A culture ingrained in Servant Leadership is not dependent on any one person or on the figure at the top. When it is woven into the fabric of the workplace it becomes a *Servant Organization*.

GROWING SERVANT LEADERSHIP IN VA

In late 2015, the National Leadership Committee voted to adopt Servant Leadership as the leadership model for the Veterans Health Administration. This is a monumental step in any enterprise, but given the size, scope and complexity of VHA, and its hierarchical/political framework, it is almost a miracle. I would love to plant the flag and declare victory, but VHA is not "there" yet. It truly is a journey and a significant benchmark has been reached. But progress is gradual, inch by painstaking inch.

Education and assessment basics were instrumental in igniting Servant Leadership in VA, but many other measures have been taken since and more are projected to nurture its growth. I believe that the present vision to become a *Servant Organization* far outstrips the original modest goals.

With the completion of the SL 360, attention was turned to a survey instrument for those who are not in formal supervisory roles. Without a "subordinate" level of raters, it cannot truly be a 360 degree assessment. It was reasoned that if we really believed *we're all leaders, all the time,* an assessment for those prospective Servant Leaders who do not have staff reporting to them was needed. Adapting the SL 360 for this group required more than minor adjustments: it had to be re-imagined to accurately reflect the realities of a non-supervisory role. One year later, the **SL 180** was released. The *yin/yang* of the SL 360 and SL 180 assessments now presents every employee in the organization an opportunity to receive meaningful data.

Servant Leader training was also kicked up a notch. Utilizing advanced technology, the Department constructed a series of electronic teaching modules with progressive curricula aimed at the new/onboarding employee on up through the executive level. Both face-to-face and online courses have been developed to accommodate an increasing number of virtual employees and alleviate the constraints of travel.

To support an informed hiring process, a Servant Leader Candidate Interview Guide was published. The Guide, organized around the Seven Pillars, contains questions for job applicants during the selection process that educe behavioral examples from the candidate's experience. Additionally, VA has designed a Servant Leader Index as part of the annual employee satisfaction survey, in order to measure the success and cultural impact of its efforts.

Perhaps one of the most ambitious undertakings has been to integrate Servant Leadership with NCOD's important work in civility, psychological safety and change management. Those concepts intuitively seem to fall under the Servant Leader rubric and are linchpins to a Servant Leader culture. Several Veterans Integrated Service Networks (VISNs) are piloting this *all things connected* approach to a healthy organization.

NCOD designed exciting new coursework around that premise.

- ✓ *Foundations* is an eight hour, online, instructor-led experience with between-session readings and action-learning assignments.

- ✓ *Skills of Servant Leadership* uses an Assessment Center format, where participants are put through a series of job-related assignments that involve decision-making, group discussion, simulated meetings, fact-finding activities and communication tasks. Trained observers and peers offer customized feedback. <u>Skills</u> is a two day course with a post-training action-learning project and telephone coaching sessions.

- ✓ *Implementing Servant Leadership in VA* is a two day tutorial on change management. Participants create and operationalize a Servant Leader change strategy in their own environment, with the assistance of expert change management coaches.

Eliciting the assistance of senior leaders across VA has been judged critical to spreading—and modeling—the message. In response, a cadre of Servant Leader Champions has emerged to reinforce efforts throughout the enterprise. These widely respected executives, volunteering outside their normal duties, will be decisive in the system-wide Servant Leadership initiative.

MEASURING THE GROWTH

I remember reading once about the Chinese bamboo tree. After planting, there is little discernable growth for the first 4 years. Then in year 5, it soars a towering 80 feet into the air. What an apt metaphor for culture! No one would say, "We have planted the seedling and if we don't see results in 12 months, we will dig it up and plant somewhere else." Rather, it would be nurtured and tended and pruned. The soil would be made ready to support it. The environment would be enhanced to sustain it. The gardeners would be trained to coax it into fullness. Success would not be measured inch by inch and month by month, but in patient and unrelenting preparation for its fruition.

Building a Servant Leader culture in VA has been much like the life-cycle of the bamboo tree. The years spent in sowing the ideas, cultivating the milieu, teaching the proprietors/caretakers, and creating the demand have been fundamental stages of growing the culture. Without that, it is too easy to walk away when conditions are less than perfect or visible results are not great enough, quickly enough.

However, in practical terms, measurable results are important. They indicate whether we're on the right path, if we're providing sufficient resources, if we've brought people on board, and how effective it is. They help us quantify systemic effectiveness and gauge satisfaction at the individual level.

Until recently, VA has methodically measured discrete attributes of Servant Leadership such as civility, psychological and physical safety, employee complaints, labor/union relationships, customer service, attrition, and the like. In addition, VA Medical Centers, VISNs and major programs have provided statistical and anecdotal outcomes stemming from Servant Leader behaviors. A few examples:

- ✓ One Medical Center reported an almost 500% reduction in Equal Opportunity complaints

- ✓ Medical Centers with the highest ratings in civility were found to have the fewest incidents of employee injury and Workers' Compensation claims

- ✓ A Regional Office dropped their claims processing time by 21 days, while improving the accuracy of their work

- ✓ Attrition dropped by 30% at one Medical Center

- ✓ Customer Service scores increased by 11% across one Veterans Integrated Service Network (VISN)

- ✓ At another VISN, engagement outcomes improved > 25%

- ✓ Fractious labor relations at several locations were transformed into true partnerships

But with the official adoption of Servant Leadership and the prioritization of the initiative, VA needed a way to measure its progress more systemically. To achieve this, a Servant Leader Index was crafted, a kind of balanced scorecard of Servant Leader factors, as assessed by VA staff in the organizations' annual All Employee Survey (AES).

The Index is constructed from 12 items selected and weighted by subject matter experts and statistical evaluation, covering 2 content areas (supervisory principles and workgroup principles), and which computes a single composite score (0–100) to measure the presence of Servant Leadership practices in the VA workplace.

The VA Servant Leader Index has been shown to substantiate:

✓ **Value to the Supervisor**

- • In higher Servant Leader environments, employees see supervisors as providing **clearer communication,** more **recognition** and more **praise**

- • In workplaces with high Servant Leadership scores, supervisors display **greater competence**

✓ **Value to the Workgroup Environment**

- VA organizations scoring high on the Servant Leader Index have workplace environments where **innovation, learning** and **speaking up** are prized

- Employees in high Servant Leader workplaces are **more satisfied with** and more likely to have **effective working relationships** with their supervisors

✓ **Value to the Organization**

- The Servant Leader Index is related to **external quality metrics**

With only two years of data collected thus far (the first year being a baseline), it is too early to measure significant culture change. VA's Servant Leader initiative is growing at a whirlwind pace, literally faster than can be documented here. It is a firm expectation that, like the bamboo tree, this assiduous groundwork and persistent progress will bring about substantial and quantifiable results in the near future.

WRAPPING UP THE PACKAGE

Every organization is unique. VA's path to Servant Leadership may not be your organization's path, but their experience is offered to you here as a gift. VA's work is produced in the public domain. Where other companies can profit from their efforts, VA's products are shared freely. VA's return-on-investment is in extending the spirit of Servant Leadership. (For further information about VA's experience and resources, including the Servant Leader Index, contact the National Center for Organization Development at **www.va.gov/ncod/**.)

Some final considerations for leaders

- Servant Leadership is countercultural and subversive in the best sense. It's an attempt to transform the established order and structure of power, authority and hierarchy.

- It does not replace traditional management functions, but shapes how they are performed. It's a fusion of *doing* and *being*.

- Servant Leadership doesn't always make things easy or comfortable. It often challenges us to think and act differently.

- Beware of executive *derailers,* behaviors that get us off track. Servant Leaders may make mistakes, but are less liable to succumb to unethical or unaccountable behaviors.

- Only you know the particulars of your job and work environment. Discern how to translate Servant Leadership into your reality.

- We are more likely to see culture change when we *live* culture change.

- Success is not a straight path. Some days you will warrant a pat on the back, others a kick in the pants. Don't be discouraged, because the goal is certain. Practice Servant Leadership: practice...practice...practice!

All Things Connected...

One July I broke my wrist while on a business trip. I expected full recovery by Labor Day, but that was not the case. The discomfort, swelling and discoloration only seemed to worsen. In a state of constant pain, I was unable to eat or sleep. And I could see no light at the end of the tunnel.

I was rescued by an Occupational Therapist, an Employee Health nurse and a surgeon who, at my worst moment, touched my shoulder and said, "We know what this is and we know what to do for it." *IT* was Reflex Sympathetic Dystrophy (RSD), a neurological complication characterized by intense pain, altered sensation and limited mobility.

My course of treatment included:

- Stellate ganglion blocks to obstruct the nerves leading to my arm

- Aggressive occupational therapy paired with integrative modalities

- A drug regimen to re-educate nerves that were confused into making pain my default state. The medications caused me to stagger and fall asleep in mid-sentence. Finding the right word or constructing a lucid thought felt like mentally wading through mud.

None of my dimensions were spared. I had to accommodate my environment to a useless right hand, was depressed at an uncertain future, anxious at being out of control. My spiritual tools seemed out of reach: I couldn't meditate through the pain. My life and my family's life revolved around illness.

In this unanticipated role reversal, I had time to consider the meaning of customer service, of patient centered care. Although I had been in health care for years, I was now pondering the greater lessons of patienthood:

- When you're in pain, *there is nothing else*

- Being a professional does not ensure competence as a patient. Even "insiders" can feel vulnerable in the health care labyrinth

- Becoming a patient is to be suddenly rendered dependent

- Don't tell me when my appointment is, ask when I can come. Don't map out my treatment for me, let me help plan the route

- Call me by my name, not my diagnosis, order in the queue or SSN. *I am not a number*

- Waiting rooms predispose to...waiting! Keep me posted on what's happening behind the scenes. Don't let me feel forgotten

- Rank has its privileges. As an executive in this health care system, I had an advantage, but VIP treatment should be the standard for all patients

- There are plenty of opportunities for customer service that don't break the budget. Courtesy, honesty, a gentle word, a caring touch and a little patience mean a lot and cost nothing

- Merging traditional and integrative therapies fosters whole-person healing. How often does a Veteran come to us with a physical complaint because he can't say, "My spirit hurts?"

- Patients don't need a lot of the clinician's time. One fully attentive moment may be enough

- Patient centered care is a *fundamental act of respect*

I am thankful that I have recovered from my ordeal. And I am grateful to have had a humbling glimpse of health care from the "other side of the bed."

An honored text says, "everything is either love or a call for love." If that is so, then our daily charge to be healers of bodies, minds and spirits is nothing less than an opportunity to love.

There is no substitute for being a patient

...All Things Connected

TOOLBOX ACTIVITY:
Servant Leader ID

⮞ Instructions ⮜

What does Servant Leadership look like? The best way to identify Servant Leader behaviors is to observe them in someone else.

Think about an historical or contemporary world leader whom you consider a Servant Leader. List as many as you can.

Now think of someone who has been a Servant Leader in your own life. List as many as you can think of.

This activity is useful in both large and small groups. See some typical responses on the next page.

⮞ Discussion ⮜

- For each person you listed, explain why you named them as a Servant Leader.

- What are the characteristics that make them Servant Leaders?

- Is there any disagreement in the group about the names listed? Why?

- Did you have more difficulty identifying Servant Leaders in your own life? Why might that be?

Use the space below to list Servant Leaders in your life

NAME	CHARACTERISTIC

TYPICAL RESPONSES / EXAMPLES	
Martin Luther King	Makes hard decisions, often at a personal cost
Mother Theresa	Inspirational
Abraham Lincoln	Makes us believe in ourselves
Mohandas Gandhi	Mission-driven
John F. Kennedy	Courageous
Florence Nightingale	Chooses to serve
Eleanor Roosevelt	Compassionate
Mother / Father	Leads by example
Clergy	Humility

VA SL 360

The following pages present a narrative version of the SL 360. It contains the VA-adapted Servant Leadership competencies, sub-competencies and ratable items. For each numbered item, the rater is instructed to indicate the extent to which they agree with the statement as a description of the person they are rating using a Likert scale (1–5, where 1 is strongly disagree and 5 is strongly agree, or Skill Not Observed.)

Raters are also given space to list two or three specific, observable behaviors where:

- The person could be more effective in demonstrating Servant Leadership

- The person is especially effective in demonstrating Servant Leadership

FIGURE 14

Pillar 1: Person of Character

Someone who maintains integrity, demonstrates humility and engages in value driven behavior.

- **Maintains Integrity**—Acts in a way that is consistent with what he/she says and thinks, is considered ethical, trustworthy and credible and values maintaining his/her integrity more than profits or personal gain

- **Demonstrates Humility**—Keeps his/her talents and accomplishments in perspective, remains other-focused, acknowledges mistakes and asks for help when needed

- **Engages in Value Driven Behavior**—Possesses clear personal core values, and uses them to guide decisions and actions

1. Can be counted on to do what she/he says she/he will do

2. Would not compromise ethical principles in order to achieve success

3. Shows that he/she is more concerned about doing what is right than looking good

4. Acts in a way that makes employees trust him/her

5. Readily admits when he/she is wrong

6. Is humble in his/her interactions with others

7. Readily shares credit with others

8. Practices behavior guided by positive values

9. Demonstrates leadership that is driven by values that go beyond his/her self-interests

Pillar 2: Puts People First

Someone who Puts People First is service driven, mentor minded and shows care and concern for others.

- **Service Driven**—Helps others even when he/she is not expected to, focuses on service to all stakeholders, including internal and external customers and goes "above and beyond" to ensure others are provided the best possible service

- **Mentor Minded**—Provides opportunity and an environment for employee growth, encourages employees to assume responsibility for their own growth and is a compassionate and wise partner in growth, while meeting others where they are

- **Shows Care and Concern**—Acts in ways that support the well-being and autonomy of employees with the intention of putting others' needs before his/her own

1. Goes above and beyond to serve others

2. Serves others willingly with no expectation of reward

3. Makes serving others a priority

4. Inspires a service-focused culture

5. Takes an active interest in employees' own goals for development

6. Works hard at finding ways to help others be the best they can be

7. Takes time to connect with employees on a personal level

8. Demonstrates the philosophy that caring about people brings out the best in them

9. Acts in a way that shows he/she cares about employees

Pillar 3: Skilled Communicator

Someone who practices empathetic listening, invites and delivers feedback effectively and communicates persuasively.

- **Practices Empathetic Listening**—Is fully present with employees, which allows for a keen awareness of their thoughts, feelings and needs, and explicitly expresses to them a deep and caring understanding of their experiences

- **Invites and Delivers Feedback**—Asks for and acts upon feedback without defensiveness, and delivers difficult feedback when necessary in a way that is honest, respectful and growth enhancing

- **Communicates Persuasively**—Guides employees to come to realizations and gain insights on their own without direct, coercive or manipulative strategies; motivates others by linking content of communication to meaningful experiences of the listener

1. Listens attentively to others

2. Seeks to understand employees' experience when listening to them

3. Delivers difficult feedback in a way that helps employees grow

4. Welcomes feedback from employees

5. Actively seeks opportunities to express deserved recognition and praise to employees

6. Communicates in a way that guides employees to come to new insights

7. Communicates in a way that inspires others

8. Connects his/her message to things that are meaningful to employees

9. Communicates in a way that relies on influence rather than positional power

Pillar 4: Compassionate Collaborator

Someone who builds teams and communities, creates a psychologically safe environment and is first among equals.

- **Builds Teams and Communities**—Encourages a culture of community that values mutual helping relationships, civility and respect

- **Creates Psychological Safety**—Creates a safe environment in which honest conversations are welcomed without fear of reprisal, employees are encouraged to come up with new ways of doing things and mistakes are not held against them

- **First Among Equals**—Promotes inclusiveness, believes employees at every level add value to the organization and de-emphasizes hierarchy

1. Encourages team members to help one another

2. Creates a sense of community at work

3. Develops an environment that supports civility

4. Creates an environment in which employees feel safe bringing up questions or concerns

5. Encourages employees to speak up within the group

6. Reacts compassionately to employees' mistakes

7. Demonstrates the belief that all employees add value to the organization

8. Treats everyone fairly regardless of their level in the organization

9. Creates an environment in which employees feel like they work with, not for, him/her

Pillar 5: Foresight

A visionary, who anticipates consequences, and takes courageous, decisive action when appropriate.

- **Visionary**—Develops and shares a compelling long-term vision, which includes employee input and connects to employees' deepest values

- **Anticipates Consequences**—Demonstrates a good understanding of what is going to happen in the future based on current information, and has a high level of intuitive insight about the way the past and present connect to the future

- **Takes Courageous, Decisive Action**—Is willing to take personal risk in the face of pressure or opposition to make the right decision for the organization; considers all aspects of the situation, including history, current data and probable impact on the future

1. Incorporates employee input in the vision for the organization

2. Articulates a compelling vision for the organization's future

3. Pays attention to emerging information that might affect the organization

4. Is skilled at anticipating the consequences of decisions

5. Balances concern for day-to-day details with the long-term success of the organization

6. Displays an understanding of how this organization's past and present connect to its future

7. Does not hesitate to take decisive action when needed

8. Takes action to shape the future rather than waiting for events to happen

9. Takes risks to do what he/she believes is right for the organization and its employees

Pillar 6: Systems Thinker

Someone who is comfortable with complexity, leads change effectively and exercises stewardship.

- **Comfortable with Complexity**—Seeks to understand as deeply as possible the interconnectedness of relationships within the larger system (between people, processes, structures, belief systems), is comfortable with this complexity and keeps this in mind when making leadership decisions

- **Leads Change Effectively**—Responds to changes faced by the organization in a flexible and effective manner, and demonstrates understanding of employees' reactions when faced with changes

- **Exercises Stewardship**—Considers the greater good when making decisions, including factors beyond the financial impact, immediate organizational goals and the individuals directly involved, looking to the future impact on both the organization and the community

1. Demonstrates a thorough understanding of how things are connected in the organization

2. Considers the impact of his/her leadership decisions on the organization as a whole

3. Effectively guides the organization through complex problems

4. Considers employee reactions to change when leading change efforts in the organization

5. Provides effective leadership in guiding changes in the organization

6. Leads by example during change efforts in the organization

7. Helps the organization contribute to the greater good

8. Helps employees see the ways in which this organization contributes to society

9. Has helped to make the organization a better place

Pillar 7: Moral Authority

Someone who shares power and control and creates a culture of accountability.

- **Shares Power and Control**—Sees every player in the organization as an important part of the enterprise and serves them by teaching, nurturing, listening and encouraging individuals and teams to take real responsibility at the highest possible levels

- **Creates a Culture of Accountability**—Sets clear performance standards in line with the organization's mission, and models behaviors consistent with this; employees are a part of setting, achieving and holding each other accountable to standards of performance.

1. Demonstrates that empowering others is important to him/her as a leader

2. Trusts employees to make decisions instead of just telling them what to do

3. Gives employees the autonomy they need to do their jobs

4. Ensures people are held accountable for the work they do

5. Works with employees to set clear performance standards

6. Models the behaviors in which employees are expected to engage

7. Encourages employees to hold each other accountable

FIGURE 14

PERSONAL DEVELOPMENT PLAN

PILLAR	PRIORITY +/-	RESOURCES	ACTIONS	REASSESS DATE
I.				
II.				
III.				
IV.				
V.				
VI.				
VII.				

FIGURE 15

❧ Chapter References ❧

Comte-Sponville, A. (2002). *A Small Treatise on the Great Virtues*. New York: Henry Holt.

Foundation for Inner Peace. (1996). *A Course in Miracles*. New York: Viking Penguin.

Longman, P. (2012). *The Best Care Anywhere*. San Francisco, CA: Barrett-Koehler Publishers.

McCarren, H., Lewis-Smith, J., Belton, L., Yanovsky, B., Robinson, J. and Osatuke, K. (2016) "Creation of a Multi-Rater Feedback Assessment for the Development of Servant Leaders in the Veterans Health Administration." Servant Leadership: Theory and Practice, Vol. 3, (1), 12-51.

Sipe, J. W. and Frick, D. M. (2009, 2015). *Seven Pillars of Servant Leadership*. New York/New Jersey: Paulist Press.

CHAPTER FIVE

All Things Connected

All Things Connected...

"Connections" are an ongoing theme of Organizational Health.

This entire chapter is dedicated to them. We can intuit connections, observe them and measure them. But is there an empirical basis for them?

Disciplines of the New Science, particularly quantum physics and cellular biology, translate scientific models to leadership and culture. So here is a scientific case for connection, from a layperson's perspective, and the lessons I have derived:

CONCEPT: CELL MEMBRANES

A cell membrane has two major functions—***protection and growth***—that are activated by hormones and proteins, and stimulated by genetic or environmental triggers. The organism (cell) can't do both at once. When it's in protection mode (a stress response), growth is impossible. Protection is always the cell's default function.

✓ **Lessons**

- This is a physiological validation of Maslow's Hierarchy of Needs: it explains why people (human organisms) cannot achieve higher level needs (love, relationship, self-actualization) when their basic survival and security needs are not met.

- If we want staff to be engaged, productive and in growth mode, it is necessary to cultivate an atmosphere of respect, fairness and psychological safety.

- It's imperative to guard against situations, systems and environments that preserve a constant state of stress. Being stuck in protection mode limits growth. Learning is chilled in a fearful environment.

CONCEPT: EVOLUTION

Gene-centric theories of evolution and growth tend to support Darwin's "survival of the fittest." In this view, genes are determinant, and competition and violence are the primary principles of survival and evolution.

Epigenesis theory regards genes as predictive, not determinant, evolving through interaction with environmental stimuli. Single cells congregate naturally to form "communities" that share similar functions. Epigenesis defines cooperation as the essential element for survival and evolution.

✓ **Lessons**

- Though we bring individual skills and experiences to our jobs, we're most effective *in community*. Teams that share tasks, goals and purpose are more likely to be successful.

- A healthy organizational culture is critical to fostering "communities of cooperation."

CONCEPT: WAVE/PARTICLE THEORY

Subatomic particles change form and properties as they respond to one another and to the scientist observing them. They form patterns of relationship that correspond to what the observer anticipates. If the observer expects to see them as a wave, they appear as a wave. If he expects to see them as particles, they appear as particles.

✓ **Lessons**

- Behaviors arise from interactions between individuals and are influenced by the environment.

- We unconsciously create the organization we expect. Literally, what we envision is what we get.

CONCEPT: FRACTAL THEORY

Fractals are patterns which replicate themselves at deeper and deeper levels. Fractals are seen at the molecular level and in nature (clouds, broccoli, ferns, etc.). While fractal components are not identical, a similar pattern or archetype is evident. (Every cauliflower floret resembles the whole cauliflower from which it comes.)

✓ **Lessons**

- Behaviors are patterned into organizations.

- Organizational macro-culture can be replicated and sustained at all levels of the organization.

- Micro-culture (work unit culture) can reflect local relevance while retaining the values of the parent organization.

CONCEPT: FIELD THEORY

Subatomic particles are situated in vast areas of space. This space is filled with non-visible fields, such as gravitational, electromagnetic and cyber fields. Scientists postulate that it's also filled with morphogenic fields: fields that influence behavior and create the culture.

✓ **Lessons**

- Think about the organizational impact of fields. Imagine customer service fields, ethics fields, team fields, and respect and engagement fields filling our workplace.

- Leaders shape fields through consistent modeling and messaging. This *is* organizational culture.

CONCEPT: MIRROR NEURONS

Mirror neurons spontaneously create brain-to-brain connections between people. They give us the capacity to assimilate the thoughts and feelings of others and to mirror others' behavior. Mirror neurons play a key role in our ability to empathize and socialize. Do you feel happier in the presence of an upbeat colleague? The mirror neuron network is the WIFI that connects us all.

✓ **Lessons**

- We understand others not by thinking, but by feeling.

- Modeling positive (or negative!) thoughts and behaviors is contagious.

- Personal contact remains important in an electronic age.

CONCEPT: NON-LOCAL PHENOMENA/ QUANTUM ENTANGLEMENT

Einstein called it "spooky action at a distance." This is the idea that two quantum particles can be so deeply linked that they share the same existence. When something happens to one, it instantaneously influences the other, regardless of the distance between them.

Spooky action travels at least four orders of magnitude faster than light. How often have people in different places come up with the same idea or invention at the same time? Have you ever answered the telephone and said, "Oh, I was just thinking about you?"

✓ **Lessons**

- Virtual employees, virtual teams may be connected in unanticipated ways.

- Thoughts and ideas are "quantum property." We sometimes call this synchronicity.

- The impact of relationships transcends time and space.

Why is all this important? These scientific roots are rich with lessons about how to lead, live and behave in the workplace.

We are connected to people, programs and the environment, sometimes in ways beyond our awareness. Like the concepts just discussed, the connections that guide, govern and move us are often unconscious and imperceptible. Many of the lessons embedded in scientific discovery are intuitive; they are just the right things to do.

There is a business case, a human case and now a scientific case for a healthy work culture. The lesson of the New Science is that they are inseparable.

...All Things Connected

Do What You Say, Say What You Mean,
One Thing Leads to Another...
—The Fixx

A healthy organization is a web of connections. At ground level we don't always see these connections. We are aware of our own space and proximate surroundings, and tend to focus there. If we work in an Emergency Room, the long-term care facility is not in our immediate field of awareness. A laboratory technician is only remotely aware of staff in the business office. We revolve in our own separate orbits.

Think, however, about how the earth appears from the window of an airplane. From that height, the people, the roads, the buildings, the green spaces, not only seem smaller, but patterns and connections emerge. A bird's-eye view of urban sprawl or wild fires or encroaching seacoasts brings home the network of our ecosystem. Beholding from the air the pyramids or Stonehenge or the Nazca lines of Peru reveals configurations that remain obscure at the surface. Seeing the big picture actually refines our focus. I believe it opens us to a kind of wisdom, an appreciation, only accessible to us from an elevated standpoint. "Zooming out" puts things into perspective.

When we observe our organizations at the 30,000 foot level we rise above our immediate circumstances. We not only see all the distinct and different parts of the organization, we perceive their commonalities and connections: we comprehend the interrelatedness of each entity to every other entity. An organization is like a jigsaw puzzle emptied out on a table: each piece is critical to the whole and until they are interlinked, the picture is not complete.

Life (and by extension organizations) is all about relationships. Meaningful work and meaningful interactions transpire at the intersections or "nodes" of relationship. While chaotic activity takes place in the interstitial spaces, those nodes of connection produce "aha" moments.

Connectivity is systems thinking, a core characteristic of Servant Leaders. Connections are present whether we acknowledge them or not, but being attentive to them gives the leader an advantage in:

- Understanding situations in their larger context
- Preventing unanticipated consequences
- Respecting the whole as greater than its parts
- Foreseeing impact/exercising foresight
- Maximizing resources and epitomizing results
- Serving colleagues and clients with reverence

Systems thinkers are able to see the *people, programs and priorities* of an organization—all at once—and keep them in perspective, can see the spatial arrangement of one to another, can trace the organization's "circulation" flow in, flow out, among and around them. Because they can see not just objects but *relationships*, the connections make sense: how a decision in one work unit affects another; how a policy can benefit one department, but impair another; how an unresolved concern today may become a crisis tomorrow.

A healthy organization is sensitive to the lightest touch. Alarms go off when programs collide, people flare and priorities clash. The prudent leader monitors the organization's vital signs so that intervention can be made before life support is needed.

PEOPLE

I recall the story of two soldiers from opposing sides who unexpectedly met face-to-face on the battlefield. They were about the same age. One had a photo of his girlfriend peeking out of his pocket. The other wore his mother's locket pinned to his lapel. They stood there surprised, frightened and suspended in time, as if seeing themselves in a mirror. In the instant they connected, they were no longer adversaries.

People are the WHO side of connection. No matter how separate we seem—or choose—to be, we are cut from the same cosmic cloth.

There is no action, no decision and no communication that does not have ripple effects. Have you ever experienced meeting a former colleague years later who thanked you for something you did or said that shaped his future? Those are truly awesome moments. It also works in the opposite direction. I was once accosted at the local mall by the wife of an employee I had terminated for patient abuse. Her rage at me reminded me that ripple effects have ever-widening repercussions. What we do touches staff, families, contractors and suppliers, stakeholders and communities.

With all things
And in all things
We are relatives.
– Dakota proverb

In a hospital or business setting, things go more smoothly when the executive and the mailroom clerk recognize their connection; when the staff in one department get along with staff in a competing department; when everyone is invested in each other's success. Sometimes, in our arrogance or thoughtlessness, we forget.

I think of the housekeeper whose job is made more onerous when visitors carelessly spill coffee in hallways. Or doctors and nurses who snap at each other in front of patients, assuming no one will notice. Patients do notice, and they worry about how the acrimony might harm their care. Or the debilitating costs of rifts between labor and management, even when their goals are in sync. Power plays on both sides tie up resources and cause disruption.

There never was a Medical Center that cured sick people by employing only nurses, nor a business that prospered with only accountants on staff, nor a college with only administrative personnel. I hire clerks as much for their congeniality as their computer skills, and physicians as much for being team players as clinical experts. Being mindful of our connection as human beings engenders civility and respect. We don't have to know, like or understand one another to appreciate that all our gifts are needed. We are *finer* together than apart.

In so many ways, the world's default paradigm is separation, not connection. At the subatomic level, though, it's the converse. Much like organizations have "fields'," so do people, an energy force that surrounds us. Throughout the workday, my field is bumping into your field and your field is overlapping someone else's field, and we merge as a kind of subatomic "semi-permeable membrane."

There are many moments when what we'd rather do is to *individuate*, to detach ourselves, times when the distance between us seems unbridgeable. Here is a technique I use, for example, in a difficult meeting, where positions are entrenched, there is dissension or even hostility, and when I am conscious of the disconnectedness of the players. Applying this mental discipline can change my internal landscape and the tenor of the meeting.

REALITY CHECK ✓

In a small group, brainstorm how many things you have in common, e.g. the same hair color, have ridden a motorcycle, or have lost a parent. In just a few minutes, you'll be amazed at how many commonalities you identify. Does finding a common bond with someone give you a new sense of connection?

The first view shows a room with discrete participants, sitting around a table with well-defined spaces around and between them. (The more divisive the issues, the wider the spaces.) The figures at the table are the focal point; separateness is the impression. Now look at the second view and see the scene in *photographic negative*: the participants fade and the space becomes the focal point. In "negative," the space no longer separates the participants, it binds them together! It becomes the field, spirit, energy or consciousness that fills the gaps between us and unites us at a quantum level.

FIGURE 16

I remember an occasion where this technique changed the outcome of an angry gathering. Several hundred frustrated Veterans were being informed that hospital beds would be closed and more convenient outpatient clinics would be established in their stead. If the Veterans had had tomatoes in their hands, I believe they would have thrown them! My first reaction was to pull back from the mob, to isolate myself physically and emotionally from the onslaught. Then as I looked out over the group, I consciously re-drew the picture, visualizing us together in a sort of bubble, surrounded by a unifying field. As my mind changed, so did my demeanor, and immediately the reactions of participants altered as well. People breathed, the tension calmed and we were able to discuss the concerns in a productive way.

PROGRAMS

In the course of a year, I receive calls from at least eight Native-American charities. Although their missions overlap, they emphatically differentiate themselves, employ competing marketing firms, make duplicative contacts to donors and struggle to meet their funding goals. I often wonder if they would be better positioned to meet their objectives, and better able to serve the Native-American population, if they were to work collaboratively toward their common purpose.

Programs are the WHAT side of connection. Apart from satisfying ego needs or assuaging nuanced points of view, there are few reasons to replicate the work. Programs that operate in collaboration are simply more effective.

Generally speaking, programs in an organization are formulated around functions that have a specific purpose and body of knowledge. Programs can become independent "fiefdoms," and some prefer it that way. That, however, is the certain road to isolation or irrelevance. To counter that, programs/program offices/program leaders must grow tentacles, send out shoots and entwine themselves in the web of connections.

To demonstrate this connectedness, what follows is a sampling of the significant programs in VA: some thoughts about the concept, its linkages to other initiatives and to Servant Leadership. Your workplace may look very different, but consider how your organization's programs may connect in ways not previously recognized.

> *It is well to remember that the entire universe, with one trifling exception, is composed of others.*
> —*John Andre Holmes*

CUSTOMER SERVICE AND
PATIENT CENTERED CARE

Certain organizations and businesses have become famous as much for their customer service as for their quality. Those companies share some beliefs and characteristics that both anchor and drive their service.

They empower employees to be fully responsible for the customer experience and give them the tools and authority to do so. Employees are engaged in systems and processes to add value, as the customer defines value. These organizations cultivate Servant Leaders at all corners of the enterprise. They take hiring and promotion seriously, have a service mindset and believe the ability to cultivate positive relationships trumps technical and professional skills.

VA has determined that customer service is not simply a training program. It is an integrated initiative that encompasses elements of exceptional service:

- A strong administrative component to define vision, principles, policy and performance expectations

- Building blocks of education, from basic courtesy training to specialized applications for clinical and professional disciplines, leadership development to establish the culture and onboarding programs to quickly acclimate new employees

- Cohesive supporting strategies from functions like Human Resources (hiring, promotion, reward and recognition), Information Technology and Informatics (measurement of service, real-time and longitudinal) and others that build customer service into the architecture of the organization

- Enculturation through the myriad Organizational Health programs and institutional priorities to highlight complementary connections and obviate a "program du jour" outlook

Servant Leadership is grounded in service. Servant Leaders create and model a philosophy of service that flows throughout the organization.

Courtesy and competence are givens: it takes much more than that to delight customers. In fact, every interaction with a customer is an opportunity to leave a positive impression. Staff are hired for attitude, trained for skills and then trusted to fulfill the charge. The organization's approach to customer service must be unified, but should never be lock-step: excellent service is always customized to the work unit and personalized to the customer.

And how do we go deeper: from service to compassion? Compassionate care and service have become the professional norm and public expectation. We don't give compassionate service because we have to, but because *we can*. We find ways to serve customers and clients even in the transactional and technological work that never touches them (phone calls, billing, records, tray lines, etc.) and that can be depersonalizing to those on both ends of the connection. How can we ensure that all our work environments support compassion?

REALITY CHECK ✓

Think of a time when you or a family member received
excellent patient care or customer service.
- What did it look like?
- How did it feel?
- Can this positive example help you to provide better service?

In VA, patients are our customers. Patient Centered Care is customer service on steroids! The ultimate customer service is based on healing relationships. To really hit the mark, Veteran customers must be satisfied with their overall *experience of care*.

VA's other customers are its employees. As demonstrated in the Transformational Model, external customer service is delivered by internal customers. Regarding staff and co-workers as customers is often a trite refrain. Hearing that "our employees are our most valuable resource" is inadequate—they must see it and feel it. We have defined power in organizations as *the capacity generated by relationships.* Servant Leaders understand that dynamic; they bring an authenticity to relationships and a vibrancy to service that honors every stakeholder.

> *Customer Service/Patient Centered Care is Connected to*: employee satisfaction, quality / performance, team effectiveness, financial health, customer loyalty

CIVILITY, RESPECT AND ENGAGEMENT

Civility matters. It matters at work, where many of us spend at least one third of our day. The quality of our work life is important. It matters in political discourse, which sets the tone for our national character. It matters at home and in the community. Civility is not only the higher moral ground, it also produces measurable outcomes.

VA's NCOD has spent years collecting data on the relationship of civility to other organizational factors, finding that higher levels of civility **decrease**:

✓ Use of sick leave

✓ EEO (Equal Employment Opportunity) complaints

✓ Recruitment costs

✓ Work-related accidents and injuries

✓ ICU (Intensive Care Unit) mortality rates and lengths of stay

And **improve**:

✓ Patient satisfaction

✓ Employee satisfaction

✓ Productivity and performance

✓ Physical and psychological safety

✓ Employees' relationship to supervisor

✓ Customer loyalty

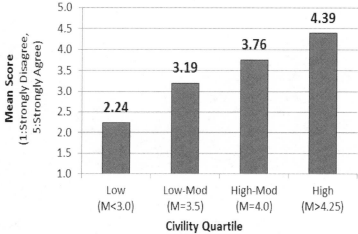

Relationship between Workplace Civility and Workgroup Psychological Safety, 2013 VA All Employee Survey, VA-wide.

All scores significantly (p<.05) different.

Civility Quartile
(Low = Bottom 25%, Moderate = Middle 50%, High = Top 25%)

FIGURE 17

CREW (Civility, Respect and Engagement in the Workplace) was VA's answer to improving work group civility. CREW was constructed to promote awareness of the importance of civility and respect among co-workers and patients, to increase the impact of civility on VA's mission and business outcomes and to raise the bar for behavior in the workplace.

CREW is a culture change initiative; it demands an organizational commitment of time, attention and support. CREW is considered a national initiative, one workgroup at a time. It is not a prescriptive agenda, but relies on a set of principles that can be actualized in locally relevant styles. It is completely acceptable that CREW may look a bit different in every VA facility. Work groups benefit from the vigorous assistance and encouragement of NCOD, but they are "taught to fish," so that CREW becomes their own venture.

CREW teaches facilitated teams and work groups new behaviors: how to have difficult conversations respectfully and constructively, to understand each other in deeper (but not personally intrusive) ways, to learn problem solving and conflict resolution skills and to have fun doing it! CREW is not a program, a project or a class: *it is the way we do business.*

Since 2005, CREW has demonstrated its effectiveness, both in NCOD data and in the articulated experiences of participants. CREW is a win-win effort, endorsed by both labor unions and managers. CREW has been taught to and its success emulated in a variety of settings in the United States and abroad. Civility and respect exemplify Servant Leader characteristics such as listening, sharing power and building community. Initiatives like CREW embody the tenet that *we're all leaders, all the time.*

(For a thorough treatment of CREW, its origins, methods and outcomes, see *Creating Healthy Workplaces*, Biron, Burke and Cooper, 2014.)

Civility is Connected to: employee and patient satisfaction, Servant Leadership, quality, safety, cost, recruitment and retention. psychological safety, high-performing teams, change management, lateral violence, systems redesign

SYSTEMS REDESIGN

Who is the most important person in airline travel? The pilot seems an obvious choice. But maybe it's the air traffic controller, who invisibly directs safe passage. Perhaps it's the navigator, who plots the best route, or the flight attendants who ensure our comfort and help in emergencies. Or these days, is it the air marshal, deterring untoward events? All these roles are important, but possibly none more than the engineer who designed the plane in the first place. Every one of those players can do their jobs to perfection, but none of that matters if the plane harbors a design flaw that will not let it do *its* job.

Design flaws that keep us from excellence are often hard-wired into processes. In health care as well as most businesses, we are constantly redesigning our work, whether we favor the popular formal redesign models or devise our own. In nature, *living systems* are ones that adapt, find new energy in new connections and function interdependently. Hopefully, your organization is a living system, where redesign is conscious, collaborative and proactive instead of an impulsive reaction to setbacks.

Redesigning a system or work process entails an appreciation of the:

- Components (organizational micro-system)
- Relationship of the components to the process (organizational macro-system)
- Relationship of the process to users/consumers (organizational ecosystem)

Done well, process redesign efforts not only solve an immediate problem or improve a product, they enable groups to discern the benefits of collaboration, innovation and meaningful communication. Teams experience a practical approach to a common goal that can simplify their work or make it more enjoyable, and they discover their collective capacity to catalyze change.

Effective redesign must incorporate systems thinking, and be multi-disciplinary in complexion. Figure 18 illustrates the actors in the redesign process. Each brings a benefit and a potential weakness to the effort.

A redesign team needs subject matter *experts*. They are the ones with thorough knowledge of the process, but they also may be wedded to the status quo. *Owners* of the process are important because they have the resources to make the change happen, but they may limit that change if their territory is threatened. Adding someone who is outside the immediate team brings *"fresh eyes"* to bear. These members are less knowledgeable about the process, but can point out details to which the team has become inured, and ask the naïve or "stupid" questions others would be hesitant to ask.

SYSTEMS THINKING & REDESIGN: UNDERSTANDING THE PLAYERS

EXPERTS	PROCESS OWNERS
-Knowledgeable	-Committed
-Status to protect	-Territory to protect

FRESH SET OF EYES	CUSTOMER/END USER
-Less knowledgeable	-Demands/expectations
-Can ask the "stupid" questions	-Final arbiter of success

FIGURE 18

The team member often forgotten is the *customer* who will be at the receiving end of the process. Customers who are astute enough to participate in redesigning an internal process, and who can suspend their personal agenda, can be hard to ferret out. But factoring in consumer demands and expectations up front can save additional redesign later. When it comes to grading the new process, the customer is the final arbiter of success.

Early in VA's systems redesign program, Rapid Improvement Teams were established across the country. Participants were enthusiastic and well trained in redesign techniques, and made impressive inroads on thorny local problems. But after their initial triumphs, some teams

encountered a slowing down of results, obstacles to consensus and unproductive interactions.

More often than not, these were complications of relationships.
Teams that had been formed on the basis of technical knowledge and
complementary skills had not had time to develop the collegial bonds
that would get them through the rough spots. In an ideal illustration
of *all things connected*, Systems Redesign and CREW found each other.
CREW staff began facilitating team practices in redesign groups, and
Systems Redesign staff taught concrete redesign methods to CREW participants, to the mutual advantage of both.

Process redesign—adding value, driving out waste—is every employee's responsibility. Time for process redesign cannot be eked out of an
already oversubscribed workday: it has to be assimilated into the work
itself. It is best accomplished by the people who use the process, not by
administrators or budgeteers. In championing redesign efforts, Servant
Leaders demonstrate *primus inter pares*, give all team members a voice,
and develop employees' fuller potential.

> *Systems Redesign is Connected to*: productivity and
> performance, fiscal responsibility, Servant Leadership, patient
> centered care, civility, learning organization, high-performing
> teams

PSYCHOLOGICAL SAFETY

Few themes demonstrate *all things connected* more convincingly than psychological safety. The ability to feel comfortable and confident in the job,
trust colleagues and leaders and know that our opinions and ideas are
valued affects everything we do at work.

W. Edwards Deming (1982), father of the quality movement,
worked with auto assembly plants. He saw it as imperative that every
worker be empowered to "stop the line" when something wasn't right.
Think about that. An assembly line is cost-effective because the parts,

pace and processes are standardized. Workers are responsible for moving a fragment of the product through their stations quickly and correctly.

But what if a defective part comes through? If allowed to proceed, the rest of the automobile is built around the defective part. On the other hand, delays are costly and not welcomed by management. The line stops and everyone down the line is idle until the problem is fixed. No employee wants to cause that kind of expensive and unpopular disruption. If the line is not stopped, however, quality, safety, customer service and public relations suffer, a more costly decision in the long run.

Deming urged that all employees, wherever they fall on the organizational chart, must be encouraged and expected to stop the line if safety or quality are compromised—a rather subversive philosophy, then and now. Writing a policy to that effect is not difficult, but creating a culture that embraces it is.

Many of us don't work on assembly lines, so how does this translate to other environments? In my work setting, for example, it could include:

- Giving feedback about a policy that might have unintended results

- Stepping in when a patient is at risk

- Respectfully disagreeing, even with someone above us in the hierarchy: speaking truth to power

- Suggesting how to improve a process

- Admitting when we've made a mistake

- Reporting an error

- Reporting a near-error

- Reporting a condition that may predispose to error

- Questioning a decision we don't understand

- Calling a *time out* at a moment of uncertainty
    o   Am I giving the right medication to the right patient?
    o   Are we about to amputate the correct leg?
    o   Will I hurt another person if I perpetuate this gossip?

- Challenging unsafe, unprofessional or unethical conduct

- Advocating on behalf of a patient

- Telling the truth, even when no one wants to hear it

These behaviors may indeed carry real or perceived risks. A psychologically safe environment provides the necessary assurances, a safe haven. *Psychological safety lives in a "field" of trust.*

REALITY CHECK ✓

What constitutes "stopping the line" in your work setting?

Psychological safety is the ability to say NO, raise questions, disagree, offer suggestions and share opposing viewpoints, without the fear of reprisal. Reprisal can include anything from being laughed at by peers to termination. Or it could be more covert: opportunities suppressed, exclusion from groups or meetings, withholding of information, being chastised in front of others, seeing someone else chastised publicly, shooting the messenger. Those acts—or simply the fear of them—dampen psychological safety.

A colleague of mine calls psychological safety the *canary in the coal mine*[9]. That's an incredibly insightful metaphor. Psychological safety is a cultural bellwether. Servant Leaders ask the difficult questions that check on how the *canary* is holding up:

- ✓ Are employees comfortable expressing their ideas, even if they're in the minority?

- ✓ Would they report a serious error, even if no one else knew?

---

9   Thank you, Maureen Cash.

✓ What in our workplace might cause employees to feel reticent about owning up?

✓ Do I always convey the impression that I want to hear about problems?

✓ How do I respond when I do hear them?

✓ Do supervisors throughout the organization encourage truth-telling?

✓ Would my employees risk telling me "the emperor has no clothes"?

✓ Do they feel sufficiently secure to engage in constructive conflict with their teams?

✓ What can I do to improve the perception of psychological safety in this organization?

Studies indicate that psychological safety goes hand-in-hand with civility, close-call reporting, crisis prevention and a learning organization. Leaders can assess the psychological safety climate through periodic anonymous and confidential employee surveys, by judicious listening, through observation and by paying attention to what *isn't* happening as much as what is.

Psychological safety is a covenant. Leaders commit to listen, keep open minds, share responsibility, invite frank discussion and appreciate differences. They do not confuse a respectful environment with a fearful one. Staff pledge to think critically, speak assertively, persist in being heard and fully engage in their work. Together they make space for human error and for people to be their authentic selves. They understand that problems identified can be resolved, and that the best way to handle a crisis is to prevent it. They strive to deserve themselves and give to each other the *gift of trust*.

Psychological Safety is Connected to: ethics, learning organizations, Servant Leadership, civility, employee satisfaction, safety, high-performing teams.

DIVERSITY AND INCLUSION

Diversity is often intertwined with the statutory function related to equal employment opportunity and legally protected groups. More precisely, it is the social imperative to reflect in its staff the people that an organization serves. Diversity provides a corporate advantage. There is a business case for diversity: teams that encompass multiple perspectives perform better on a number of indicators. Inclusion takes this a step further, enabling full participation of *all* individuals in the organization.

We each develop mental models that form our expectations of what people or things "should be." Maybe you visualize a man with a stethoscope and lab coat when you think of a doctor, but what if the doctor is a university professor? Or the nurse you expect to be female turns out to be a Hispanic male? Or the CEO you pictured as a middle-aged man is actually a young woman? Have you ever heard someone say, "You don't act like a minister," "You don't look like a grandmother," or "He doesn't sound like a politician?" When the *actual* is different from our mental model, our brains are forced to do an instant recalibration to match what we expected to see with what is in front of us.

Our experiences frame our mental models, and so does our language. There is something that sounds more serious about an *usher* than an *usherette,* for example. (The dictionary defines 'ette' as "less than; a cheap imitation of, as in leather/leatherette".) And when we refer to a judge, a firefighter or an executive as *he*, and a nurse, teacher or secretary as *she*, does it sway how we think about the person's capabilities? Does it color our expectations? Does it influence whom we hire? Being inclusive in our language is not just an issue of political correctness: it opens windows of perception and possibility. *Language matters.*

Diversity takes us broader; inclusion takes us deeper. Servant Leaders give everyone a seat at the table. Listening and communication skills help Servant Leaders to see past surface appearances; humility leads them to recognize their own unconscious biases.

Diversity and Inclusion are Connected to: Servant Leadership, productivity/performance, employee satisfaction, ethics, civility, respect, high-performing teams

CHANGE MANAGEMENT

Managing change sounds like an oxymoron. Change is persistent and perpetual. When the organization adopts a new philosophy, new procedures, new technology, or transitions to a new leader—especially if all this is occurring at once—it can leave us feeling a loss of control. Often we attempt to wrest back that control by resisting the change.

Change is resisted actively or passively. I can loudly reject the change or simply wait it out. Change is a process that travels through stages of resistance and acceptance. We know that acceptance is reached sooner and more tolerably when the people who will have to live with the changes are involved in planning them, and when the change is assertively and intentionally *managed*. Many tools and formal methods exist to guide the management of change.

Employees accept and support change that makes sense and is communicated clearly, and Servant Leaders have an edge here. Many of the principles and characteristics of Servant Leaders lend themselves to managing change and facilitating acceptance:

- Servant Leaders ensure that staff is involved, throughout the process and at all organizational levels. They enlist everyone in the change.

  If you don't like change, you're going to like irrelevance even less.
  —Eric Shinseki

- Change is more likely to occur when psychological safety is high. Servant Leaders are open to feedback, listen and reflect. They communicate via many modalities and at every occasion.

- Change is initiated for the right reasons and executed in the right way.

- Servant Leaders foresee and finesse the cultural implications of change.

- They share credit when the change goes well; they share concern, but not blame when it doesn't.

- Change is not a light switch; it's an ongoing process. Servant Leaders remain open to tweaking along the way, course-correcting when necessary, because the *change is not ego-based*.

Every person cannot weigh in on every decision around the change, but finding opportunities for them to influence even minor decisions pays dividends. Can the employee choose what color to paint his office? Help plan the physical layout and flow of an area? Test equipment and furnishings for spatial fit? Determine how the work space will be arranged? Even small choices confer a measure of inclusion and control.

In exercising foresight, the Servant Leader understands the essential factor of timeliness in guiding change. *Propitious* change is change whose time has come. It is a confluence of external acceptability, internal capacity and values. We have experienced many changes in our lifetime that simply required the right timing to gain a foothold—everything from Civil Rights to smoking policies.

A modest health care change, patient visiting norms, comes to mind. When I was a student, families were on the periphery of their loved one's care. Visiting hours were sacred, expectant fathers paced outside delivery rooms, families waited in assigned areas, children were never allowed in the patient room and the Infection Control nurse would have fainted to see a pet in the hallway! Today, all members of the family, often including pets, are encouraged to visit liberally. So what *permitted* the shift?

The environment was favorable; things fell into place.

- External limitations were relaxed: laws, rules, protocols; new data related to transmission of disease and the positive impact of families on healing; adapting social acceptability and expectations.

- Internal capacity was achieved: conducive space was designed for families, recliners in the patient room, designated shower and kitchen facilities, food service, labor and delivery suites, in-hospital child care, valet parking, etc.

- Most importantly, the changes were congruent with evolving organizational values: family participation, privacy, holistic health, patient centered care, transparency, shared accountability, inclusion and customer service.

When leading change, Servant Leaders weigh and balance those environmental factors, discerning when it is best to respect the parameters, and when it is *propitious* to demolish them.

Changes, especially transformational changes that will affect the culture, require great sensitivity. Work groups that have established their culture over time can experience a sense of loss. I recall a nursing unit that was planned for closure; the staff would be absorbed into other units. The unit had a shared identity unique to its distinct function and close relationships of the individuals who worked there. The new unit would be larger and more modern, but less personal and not amenable to their routines and customs.

The staff was given permission to grieve. They decided to hold a wake for the "moribund" unit. They wrote and recited eulogies. They "buried" mementos of their time together in a cardboard box. They said their goodbyes to the things they would miss most, and laughed about all the silly and happy memories. They closed out the past. And then they brought a part of it into their future. A small statue of a hospital benefactor that had been ensconced on the old unit was ceremoniously carried along to the new unit, symbolically integrating the two cultures as well.

Change Management is Connected to: Servant Leadership, employee satisfaction, learning organization

ETHICS

Ethics is doing the right thing *when no one is looking*. It embodies the principles of:

- ✓ Autonomy: Respect for individual freedom of choice
- ✓ Non-maleficence: Do no harm to others

- ✓ Beneficence: Do good and prevent harm
- ✓ Justice: Fair treatment according to needs; fair distribution of resources
- ✓ Fidelity: Loyalty, faithfulness, honoring commitments made

In a hospital setting, ethics are usually interpreted in a clinical context, e.g., when to "pull the plug," or ration health care, but they extend to giving the right/efficacious treatment, and granting the patient a voice in decision-making.

So much of ethics has to do with leadership: how budget is allocated, adequacy of staff and equipment, not cutting corners, integrity of decisions, transparency of communication, owning up to errors and correcting them. Leaders can best mitigate ethical problems by preventing them, creating a culture where truth-telling is honored, where ethical "glitches" are remedied and everyone is accountable for an ethical climate.

Greenleaf posited that Foresight, a key Servant Leader attribute, is also an ethical obligation. Simply put, foresight is "skating to where the hockey puck will be," understanding enough about what is on the horizon—in the industry, society, politics, economics, etc.—to intuit what the impact might be on the leader's environment. The ethical side of foresight speaks to the fiduciary duty of the leader to safeguard the interests of the organization.

When organizational ethics lapse, they can run the gamut from deliberate breaches, to errors of perception and unintended consequences, to true ethical dilemmas. Think of these lapses in the image of a thermometer, where we are taking the "temperature" of organizational ethics.

In terms of managing them, deliberate breaches of ethics are often cut and dried, and frequently illegal as well as unethical. A hospital example is employee theft of drugs: not only illegal, but a violation of professional and patient ethics. I assign this lapse to the *cold end* of the thermometer, even though it's a major breach, because once corroborated,

there are prescriptive formal processes to address it. Handling this situation is serious, but the protocols are well defined.

Next on the thermometer in terms of "heat" are the *unintended consequences* of systems and processes. Perhaps a system has a design flaw that results in increased human error, or a policy forces staff to take shortcuts that compromise patient safety. This is an example of best laid plans going awry. The strategies and actions here are more complicated because the problems were not anticipated. Here leaders need to observe and listen, reward the identification of close calls, recognize the anomaly explicitly, and then engage in resolution or redesign.

"Warmer" yet are perceptual lapses colored by the work environment or culture. Organizations that stress data and performance metrics, for example, can unwittingly create the perception that scores, not service, are the goal.

Have you ever heard a leader encourage staff to "do whatever it takes"? Be cautious how such statements are interpreted. Well-meaning employees have been known to falsify records or "massage" rules to meet that challenge. To avoid this trap, leaders should reiterate the underlying values, be transparent in communication and ask the clarifying question, "What do you hear me saying?"

The weather conditions for true ethical dilemmas are *hot and humid*: they make the leader sweat! They are related to decisions and actions and are the most complex. There may not be only one right answer: there may not be *any* right answer, perhaps only a better choice.

These situations require structured devices such as an Ethics Board, ethics "climate" surveys, a Framework for Ethical Decision-Making (see Figure 19 for a prototype), an anonymous internal ethics advice line accessible to all staff and an "ethics monitor" at meetings who alerts participants to ethical implications of the discussion.

Ethics is Connected to: Servant Leadership, learning organization, psychological safety, culture, employee satisfaction

PRIORITIES

Physicians at a Medical Center were incentivized to meet certain clinical performance goals. Among these goals were: achieving 100% of patients vaccinated against flu and pneumonia and 100% of patients reporting that they were given the opportunity to participate in their care decisions. The physicians soon realized that these were competing priorities. A patient who declined inoculation would earn them a plus on one side of the scorecard, but a minus on the other. Unless all patients agreed to vaccination, the physician would never merit the incentive. While both goals were laudable, the conflict created confusion, inconsistency and in some cases ethical issues for the practitioners.

> *Priorities are the HOW side of connection. Too many, ambiguous, shifting, or conflicting priorities actually subvert the connections between people and programs. Priorities that are lucid, comprehensible, and value-based forge connections between people and programs. Clear priorities are a roadmap for meeting the mission.*

All organizations want to interface with people and administer their programs in a manner that is faithful to their professed mission and values. Most official values statements include attributes like integrity, trust, compassion, respect, excellence and stewardship. Such sentiments are noble, but hollow, unless leaders manifest them through their organizational priorities. For employees to ascribe to those values and assimilate them into their work, the leader must demonstrate them *visibly* in the priorities of the organization. Some of those priorities might include:

- *Quality/Performance/Safety/Cost or Value* are the cornerstones of most organizations, the most basic goals of an enterprise. More precisely, they are *outcomes* of a Servant Leader culture and direct beneficiaries of an *all things connected* environment.

- *Employee Satisfaction* or being an *employer of choice.* The goal is not to make everyone happy: it is to help them be engaged and fulfilled, to feel they are making a contribution, to understand their personal connection to the mission of the organization. Why is it important that they are here? How are their unique gifts honored?

- *High Performing Teams*—all workgroups are not teams. Teams work together toward the same goal, efficiently in their work functions and effectively in their work relationships, complement each other's abilities, shore up each other's weaknesses and encourage each other to greatness.

- *Succession Planning* is a thoughtful pathway to ensure that every generation of leadership builds upon the achievements of the last, that the leadership pipeline is diverse, that leaders are well prepared to meet the physical, emotional and ethical challenges at every step.

- *Learning Organization*—an enterprise that values learning, allocates time and resources to learning and furnishes learning opportunities. More significant yet, the organization—as a living system—learns from its own mistakes, crises, accomplishments and innovations. It doesn't repeat its errors or relive its humiliations. It does critique and rectify its failures, extrapolate wisdom and generalize learning. Learning organizations honor the lessons of the past, attain a systemic maturity of judgment and ensure strong legacies.

- *Servant Leadership* offers a structure that puts people, programs and priorities into context. It is the *constitution* of the Organizational Health Umbrella. Although Servant Leadership is often presented as a program, it is more precisely the "big picture" construct encompassing everything else.

And I do mean everything. If there comes a time that you lay Servant Leadership aside, justify a situation where Servant Leadership "doesn't pertain," put it on hold until you're in a more conducive job, your internal warning bells should start clanging. The behaviors and characteristics your organization rewards may bear little resemblance to the behaviors and characteristics of a Servant Leader. If that's the case, there may be choices to make. Servant Leadership is always a conscious decision.

FORGING THE LINKS

Using VA's experience as a guide, the goal of this chapter was to shine a light on the infinite connections in all our organizations and why those connections are important. Much like culture, connections can be ignored, or they can be managed and encouraged. People, programs and priorities are linked in profound and enlightening ways, and finding their relatedness can reap huge returns.

The savvy leader makes a habit of soaring at 30,000 feet, i.e., seeing the big picture, in order to monitor the patterns and relationships that make or break an organization.

As people connect, they learn to care about each other. As programs connect, their impact burgeons. As priorities connect, the path forward becomes clear.

To me, "all things connected" is not just a snappy tagline: it is a truth. What I do and how I do it, what I say and how I say it, what I decide, what I plan, how I interact, how I lead and what I model—all can reverberate in ways known and unknown, now or in the future, for better or for worse. Those connections exist, whether or not we recognize them. By helping employees and colleagues understand them, Servant Leaders foster a holistic, interdependent and flourishing workplace.

*   *   *

FRAMEWORK FOR ETHICAL DECISION-MAKING

This Framework is intended as a guide to help employees make decisions. Decision-making can sometimes be very difficult, especially when there is not a policy or work rule to govern the situation or there is more than one possible "right" answer. At times like this, ethical dilemmas occur.

The purpose of this tool is to enable any staff member or senior manager to think critically about situations and craft ethical, effective, value-driven and timely decisions that are in alignment with values and goals. Please read the instructions below and follow the steps.

1. State the situation or problem that compels the need for a decision. What is the ethical dilemma? Who are the stakeholders? What is their role and interest?

2. Identify options to deal with the situation as defined above. There are at least two options in every situation, one of which is to do nothing.

    1.

    2.

    3.

3. Evaluate all options generated using the grid on the next page for each.

	OPTION 1		OPTION 2		OPTION 3	
	YES	NO	YES	NO	YES	NO
Does this violate any known laws or regulations?						
Is there personal gain?						
Is there misuse of position?						
Is there a conflict of interest						

If the answers to all questions are NO, proceed to the next step. If the answer to any of the questions is YES, reconsider your options.

4. Consider Values, Goals and Ethical Principles for each of the options.

	OPTION 1			OPTION 2			OPTION 3		
	Support	Neutral	Conflict	Support	Neutral	Conflict	Support	Neutral	Conflict
VALUES									
Integrity									
Commitment									
Advocacy									
Respect									
Excellence									
Trust									

	OPTION 1			OPTION 2			OPTION 3		
	Support	Neutral	Conflict	Support	Neutral	Conflict	Support	Neutral	Conflict
GOALS									
Quality/Reliability									
Access									
Function									
Customer Service (internal & external)									
Patient Centered									
Cost and Value									
Community Health									
ETHICAL PRINCIPLES									
Autonomy: Respecting individual freedom of choice									
Non-malefi-cence: Do no harm to others									
Beneficence: To do good and prevent harm									
Justice: Fair treatment according to needs; fair distribution of resources									
Fidelity: Loyal, faithful, honoring commitments made									

5. Select the most desirable or optimal option.

6. Are there organizational barriers or political considerations in implementing this option? If so, how will these be dealt with and resolved?

7. Develop an action plan to implement your decision. Who needs to know this decision and how will it be communicated? How will it be implemented?

8. How will results be evaluated and in what timeframe?

FIGURE 19

All Things Connected...

Psychological safety is a significant factor in employee engagement, and there are hard data that connect it to civility, customer satisfaction, quality and physical safety as well.

Psychological safety is not just a good feeling, it is a product of trust and plays out in critical ways: building effective teams, "stopping the line" when health and well-being are threatened, delivering bad news, suggesting improvements, taking creative risks, etc.

These situations require trust between supervisor and staff, and among colleagues. The absence of psychological safety can result in consequences ranging from personal detachment to organizational crisis.

The hypothetical basis for poor psychological safety is *power differential*. When power is derived from positional authority, someone always has more and someone always has less. The degree of perceived power is directly related to the box on the organizational chart, the number of staff supervised, the budget dollars controlled or who one knows.

On a recent weekend, I watched two programs that spoke profoundly to me about the true nature of power. The first was *Gandhi*. While educated in England, Gandhi had no standing in his own country, which was under British colonialism, yet he turned the tide for Indian independence. He did this by waging a war where the arms were persistence, persuasion, humility and non-violence. This unconventional strategy had a profound effect on his persecutors and compatriots alike. When asked why he prevented his followers from retaliating, he answered that "an eye for an eye only makes the whole world blind."

The second program was a documentary about Father Jerzy Popieluscko, a Polish priest who championed the Solidarity movement during the Communist regime. His growing popularity with the oppressed Polish people put him increasingly at odds with the military and secret police. Like Gandhi, Father Popieluscko's weapons were love, truth, courage and a living example. Even after his brutal torture and murder, his adherents honored his teachings of peaceful non-cooperation.

Mohandas Gandhi and Jerzy Popieluscko, like Mother Teresa, Martin Luther King, Jr., Malala Yousafzai and others, understood that their approach was revolutionary in the truest sense. These leaders did not assert positional power, but their power to move, inspire and transform is indisputable. *Theirs was the power inherent in human dignity.* They did not claim power for themselves: they extended it to friends and adversaries alike.

Many speculate that our traditional hierarchical structures have cultivated in their workers a "learned helplessness." But anything that is learned can be unlearned.

Equilibrating the power differential is not a matter of hierarchy, it's a matter of heart. It is unacceptable to remain quiet when something is wrong or when someone has been wronged. It's counterproductive to engage in divisiveness and reprisal. It's beneath us to promote bitterness and conflict. Only people who do not recognize—or do not claim—their own intrinsic power, play in that muck. Psychological safety and personal accountability are joined at the hip.

Most of us will not achieve the stature of a Gandhi, and our causes are much more modest, but we need the Gandhis to remind us of our own potential. How many Gandhis are in our midst? How many Mother Teresas work alongside us every day? They are all around us if we only have the eyes to see them.

When we encounter the wrong use of power, how do we respond? Do we ignore it, hoping it will go away, give back as good as we get or confidently and compellingly affirm our own truth?

The power differential may be more artifact than fact. We must not use it as an impediment to being fully who we are. And it shouldn't prevent us from reaching out to whomever we believe to be on the other end of our own personal power equation. They, too, need our compassion.

People with power are not always Servant Leaders, but Servant Leaders are always people of power.

...All Things Connected

TOOLBOX ACTIVITY:
Webs of Connections

☙ Instructions ❧

Healthy organizations are *webs of connection*. On the next page is a diagram of a web. Think of some of the programs or priorities in your organization that may have elements of connection. Write them in the spaces provided. Feel free to add more spaces if you need them. Consider the way your programs link: what connects to what else? Draw lines to join them.

☙ Discussion ❧

1. Do any of the linkages surprise you? Which ones?

2. Had you recognized the connections before?

3. If you are in a group, did others have different results?

4. Talk about the specific elements of connection between each shape you connected. How could the programs enhance each other?

5. Are there any patterns?

6. How will you make it a practice to identify the connections in your organization?

❧ Chapter References ❧

Biron, C., Burke, R. J. and Cooper, C. L. (2014). *Creating Healthy Workplaces*. Surrey, England: Gower Publishing.

Capra, F. (1991). *The Tao of Physics*. Boston, MA: Shambala Press.

Deming, W. E., (1982). *Out of the Crisis*. Cambridge, MA: The MIT Press.

Holmes, J. A., www.quotationspage.com

Keith, K. M. (2013). *The Ethical Advantage of Servant Leadership*. Singapore: The Greenleaf Centre for Servant Leadership (Asia).

Lipton, B. (2007). *The Biology of Belief*. New York City: Hay House.

Emerging Technology from the arXiv. "Chinese Physicists Measure Speed of "Spooky Action at a Distance'." MIT Technology Review, March 7, 2013.

Perry, S. (2008). Society for Neuroscience, Nov. 16.

Shinsecki, E. (2001). www.brainyquotes.com

Wheatley, M. (2006). *Leadership and the New Science*. San Francisco, CA: Berrett-Koehler.

CHAPTER SIX

Humanagement

All Things Connected...

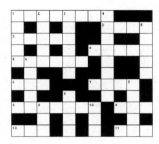

Words are powerful tools. They reflect our feelings and influence our behavior. Words shape the way we perceive the people we serve.

In a health care setting, *Veteran*, *Patient*, *Customer*, *Client*—each term describes a different relationship between the giver and receiver of care. Clinical professionals are loathe to use the word *customer*, but we need to rethink the significance of that label. When we are given marginal service in a store or restaurant, we're quick to ask, "Who's the customer here?!" We all know the adage that the customer is always right. We want to be served quickly and respectfully, trust the quality of the product and the skill of the provider, have our preferences and expectations met and anticipate the business will go the extra mile to retain our loyalty.

Health care is surely different from business, but "patient customers" seek the same service.

In a highly competitive health care environment, patients/customers *make choices,* sometimes based on reputation and clinical "scorecards," but more often on the quality of relationships and their *experience of care.*

I tell the story of my aunt, a World War II Veteran, who developed bone cancer and underwent several amputations at a VA facility. She was an important role model in my life and I was increasingly distressed by her lack of progress. In desperation I called and pleaded with her to transfer to a private hospital or a university hospital. "You can get care anywhere you choose!"

Her response was sobering: "You don't see. *I am where I choose to be.* These people understand me and care for me."

I'll never know if my aunt received the finest quality of care, but I know *absolutely* that it was her perception that she did. Being the best is not just measured in data or performance metrics, but first and foremost in the estimation of our customers.

Let me add another term to our list: *guest*. The concept of *customer* is tied to satisfaction; the concept of *guest* is linked to hospitality. Don Berwick of the Institute for Health Care Improvement reminds us that all caregivers are *guests* in the lives of their patients.

Henri Nouwen (1975) offers these insights (paraphrased) on hospitality:

The term "hospitality" should not be limited to its literal sense of receiving a stranger in our house; it is a fundamental attitude toward fellow human beings.

Those in the helping professions have to keep reminding themselves that they do not own those in need of care. The danger inherent in the professionalization of healing is that it becomes a way of exercising power instead of offering service.

Patients may view those who are helping them with fear and apprehension. Doctors, nurses, chaplains, psychologists, social workers, are looked up to as if they were endowed with mysterious powers. They accept that these professionals may say things that cannot be understood, do things that cannot be questioned and make decisions about their lives with no explanation.

Every human being is called upon to be a healer. In an age of specialization, we tend to underestimate our own healing potential. We are all healers who can reach out to offer health, and we are all patients in constant need of help. Only this realization can keep professionals from becoming distant technicians and those in need of care from feeling used or manipulated.

Careful listening and a full, real presence to each other is one of the highest forms of hospitality. As healers, we must keep striving to create a space in which we all connect as fellow travelers sharing the same human condition and a common destination.

...All Things Connected

We Are Family...
—Sister Sledge

My father taught English at the high school I attended. (We won't get into the obvious complications!) His female students were always falling in love with him, and Maura was no exception. But Maura was different. She was small and unattractive, a below average student and blind. She was not popular. Perhaps because of her disability, she was needy and clinging; she had no social graces and was just not pleasant to be around. And so students avoided her and teachers ignored her.

Except my father. My father was not a touchy-feely kind of man. He was fairly detached with most students, but Maura somehow worked her way past his defenses. Besides intercepting him throughout the school day, she developed a habit of calling him at home...every night...during dinner. This went on for weeks and whenever she phoned, he left the table and talked with her.

I have to admit I was not a Maura "fan," and I couldn't fathom my father's willingness to let her repeatedly interrupt a family meal. One evening, in a fit of impatience, I confronted him. "Why don't you just not answer the phone? Why are you always listening to her?" Why do you let her use up your time?"

"Because that is what she needs," he replied.

Such a simple, but poignant response and, I thought, uncharacteristic. And then 20 years later I was leading a state hospital system, where one of my employees, Dr. Mike, set up an appointment to see me. And then another, and another, in fact a couple of times a week. We would finish our work conversation in short order, then he would pull out pictures of his family or bring in some of his poems to share with me. My schedule was hectic and I often found myself wishing he would wrap it up.

One day my secretary approached me and said that the next time Mike asked, she would make excuses for me. She was trying to help me manage my schedule. When I declined her offer, she said, "I don't know why you let him use up your time like that!" Instantaneously I heard my father's voice in my head. "Because that is what he needs," I answered.

In many contemporary organizations, it is more about what the manager needs than what the employee needs. In fact, meeting the latter often goes a long way toward meeting the former.

Management is defined as the conducting or supervising of something, the judicious use of means to accomplish an end. We often contrast management—the hard skills of planning, implementation, execution and oversight—with leadership—the art of getting things done through people. The truth is that leaders must be adept at both: they have to know how to manage the work and they have to motivate and inspire people to accomplish the work.

Years ago I coined the neologism Humanagement to express the dual nature of leadership. Humanagement is a concept that serves to counteract our tendency to euphemize or depersonalize the hard skills. It reminds us that the human side of decisions, actions and interactions comes first. As leadership ideologies, Humanagement and Servant Leadership seem to be very much in harmony.

There is a difference between being in a leadership position and being a leader. Through the years I have known people in leadership positions who had all the outward trappings of power, but were incredibly ineffectual or struggled inordinately to get ahead, and those who claimed success in terms of wealth or authority, but had little real influence or lasting impact.

I recall an iconic executive who attracted all the top talent but burned them out within a year, a brilliant surgeon with cutting edge ideas that never came to fruition because no one wanted to work with him, a department head who was so afraid to engage with staff that he became a literal

> *No company or organization filled with unhappy people will ultimately rise to its highest potential.*
>
> – Marianne Williamson

prisoner in his "ivory tower." I have encountered top leaders who come to the post confident that they can "fix" the organization, turn it around, then are incredulous that subordinates don't rush to conform, that they have minds of their own and that the organizational "fixes" are much more complex than they anticipated.

Each of these examples in its own way forgot the covenant of employer and employee, lost track of the human side of management.

THE MYTH OF CONTROL

In the context of *Humanagement,* control is corrosive at worst, an illusion at best. Events can be managed, people can be supervised, but some things are simply beyond the leader's control. The Alcoholics Anonymous prayer can be adapted here: Grant me the serenity to accept what I cannot control, the courage to control what I can, and the wisdom to know the difference!

The myth of control is founded on a variety of premises—all of them dangerous:

- An assumption that a leader must know everything

- An assumption that if something goes wrong, it's the leader's failure

- A culture in which failure is not permitted

- A strategy of separation or isolation
- Ego, fear, emotional woundedness and other "personal baggage"

Examples of leaders' destructive attempts to control abound:

- The leader who gave many people fragments of information but gave no one "big picture" information
- A supervisor who limited collaboration by requiring that staff obtain her consent to make contacts outside a strict chain of command
- The manager who enjoyed keeping people off balance: what was rewarded one day was punished the next; an employee could be favored today and shunned tomorrow
- A director who used public humiliation to control the dissent of staff
- The president of a two-hospital merger who forbade department heads at one facility from collaborating with their counterparts at the other facility

Workers can, and indeed have, tolerated abuse from managers in the guise of tight management or administrative control. In a study at one organization, more than two thirds of employees reported having experienced verbal abuse or bullying from a supervisor during the year of the study. Examples included name-calling, ostracism, malicious gossip, public ridicule or scolding, withholding of key information, being shouted at, etc. Sadly, many of the respondents accepted this treatment as just part of the job! The American workplace has become much better over the last decades about curbing and preventing physical violence at work, but may be becoming more adroit at doing violence to the spirit.

Employees become accustomed to being ignored, neglected or over-tasked. The expression "whippin' the mules and grazin' the ponies" has been used to describe supervisors who load work on staff they know will do the job and let others off the hook. People in a work unit know who the mules and the ponies are!

Employees can be coerced into action or cowed into submission for a time, but they will look for a way out and will bring only a shadow of themselves to the job until they find that way out. They will do only what they are forced to do, offer nothing of their intellect or enthusiasm, become neatly disengaged. Some will actively sabotage, find ways to quietly circumvent or retire in place.

Despite the travesties of management, people are also quick to forgive. I marvel at how employees can rebound from a bad supervisor when they experience a good one. I have witnessed complete turnarounds in work units where the supervisor has "converted" to Servant Leadership, often surprising both the supervisor and staff. Although traditional work environments have taught us over time to tolerate managers' misguided efforts at control and other misbehaviors, the resilience of "the managed" is nothing short of amazing.

* * *

Remember that real power in organizations has little to do with position or status, how many employees are supervised or how many budget dollars are at one's disposal. In healthy organizations, *real power is the capacity generated by relationships.* Relationships are the *real work* of an organization. We must be careful that the important *tasks* leaders do—running a company, balancing a budget, planning strategies, marketing a product, meeting performance goals, etc.—do not become a distraction from the *real work of relationships.*

> *The trouble with coercive power is that it only strengthens resistance.*
>
> – Robert K. Greenleaf

I abhor the saying, "Don't take it personally; it's just business." Such a casual way to disregard the human impact of business decisions! A colleague of mine was faced with downsizing a long-term care facility she had overseen for a decade. The action, based on financial realities and by legislative mandate, would put residents out of their homes and employees out of their jobs. It was probably a sound business decision, but the human impact could not just be written off.

Similarly, organizational decisions may be tacitly saying, "Don't take it personally, it's just management." There is nothing impersonal about freezing salaries, abolishing jobs, firing (even for cause), shutting down a department, forcing overtime and on and on.

Hear this: *good* managers take these actions all the time. They are often justified, responsible and necessary in fulfilling their promise of stewardship. If the ship is sinking, you toss the deck chairs overboard; if an employee abuses patients or threatens co-workers, you terminate him. But as necessary as those actions may be, they should never be performed lightly. I believe that the better the manager, the tougher those decisions are. They must be undertaken with a gravitas that acknowledges the human impact. I know CEOs who deliver disciplinary actions with such compassion that the employees thank them.

An administrator once confessed that letting an employee go was one of the hardest things she had to do. "Even when I'm absolutely sure it's the right decision, it still grieves me." "I would worry if it didn't," I replied.

Another leader has a rule of thumb for well-meaning employees who are unable to correct performance deficits or conduct difficulties after repeated counseling. "When we both know it just isn't going to work out, we agree on a date of separation and I give them 'safe passage' until then. It's not a license to goof off, but it allows them some time to find a new job and softens the stress of being terminated."

Leadership is difficult, consuming work. It is the leader's role to make the onerous and fateful decisions. *Humanagement* does not deflect us from that responsibility, but it sensitizes us to the human implications. Maybe we should all wear a label: "*Handle with Care*." Servant Leaders, *Humanagers,* take the consequences of their actions *very* personally.

WHAT DO YOU NEED?

I have attended many retreats and workshops during my career, but one of them (Oshry, Organization Workshop) included an exercise that has stuck with me. Participants were divided into three groups: *tops,* which represented senior executives, *middles,* which were mid-level supervisors and *bottoms,* or front-line staff. I was designated a *middle.* My group was charged with selecting a project that could benefit our mythical work-place, persuading the *tops* to support it, then presenting it to the *bottoms.*

We decided to develop a package of recruitment and retention perks for front-line staff. I'm hazy on the specifics, but I remember the package included some additional paid time off, childcare benefits and tuition reimbursement for college courses related to the job. (I do believe we were more creative than that, but you get the idea.)

Selling the package to the *tops* was not difficult since we were able to suggest sources for capitalizing the project and to calculate a reason-able return on investment. What surprised me (and the lesson that has remained with me) was that the *bottoms* were not happy. They did not fall over themselves with thanks. Really?! How were they not grateful? We had done this for them!

But had we…? Those without children inquired if we had consid-ered elder care; some felt that with more time off, their work would just pile up and make the job harder when they came back; others asserted they would rather go to a self-improvement class than enroll in a college course. They wondered if we had thought about job sharing, reward and recognition programs, team performance bonuses and the like. We had not. We presented the package as *fait accompli.* We had never thought to ask them what they would find useful.

Remember Maura and Dr. Mike, who needed a little time, some undivided attention? Others may need a challenging assignment, a word of appreciation, a salary increase, a smile, a sabbatical, more responsibil-ity, an afternoon off to watch a child's baseball game, some help with an aging parent. The needs are as varied as the people in the organization.

As a novice supervisor, I maintained what I called Employee Care Plans (see Figure 22), a variation on Patient Care Plans that guide the course of nursing care. I would interview new staff about what was important to them, what motivated them, what work issues turned them off, their aspirations, the legacy they hoped to leave, how they wanted to be known, their talents and what they needed from me. We would revisit that conversation at least once a year to check on how well we were following the Care Plan.

Some of my peers were shocked at that approach, predicting that employees would make unrealistic or outrageous requests, but that never happened. Staff were not only reasonable, they were grateful that their supervisor was expressing an interest. Merely having the conversation strengthened our relationships.

How do managers know what people need? *They ask.*

FAMILY MATTERS

Many organizations see their constituents as *family*. VA is one of those, but I never really understood that until a VA leader in my hometown—someone I had never met—came to my mother's funeral. His presence seemed to me an overwhelming act of solidarity. And then there was the instance when a supervisor helped pack up an employee's belongings as he moved back home to die. And when a clerk at a VA hospital paid for a patient's ride home out of her own pocket so he could spend the weekend with his family. And when a retiree flew to another state to share a co-worker's celebration. Every workplace has such stories and, over time, they become "cultural cues," a kind of organizational mythology.

Family dynamics being what they are, squabbles and rifts are bound to occur. In organizations, we can either choose to disagree respectfully and use conflict creatively, or we can face frequent dissension and break into factions. *We/They* mentalities run amok in workplaces: management vs labor, physicians vs nurses, caregivers vs support staff, psychiatrists vs psychologists, baby boomers vs millennials, political appointees vs career bureaucrats, corner office folks vs cubicle dwellers and so many others.

A senior manager I had agreed to coach was fretful about an upcoming meeting. Her department had encountered a systems glitch that was continuing to generate unhappy customers, and she was being pressed by her boss to facilitate a timely resolution. The manager called together her direct reports, a multi-disciplinary group of supervisors, each of whom was responsible for one facet of the problem. She had put forth the challenge, hoping for an interactive process redesign session, but what she got was a circling of the wagons. Although each group member had a role in finding the solution, no one took ownership of the problem. Instead, everyone was busy defending their turf and pointing a finger at one another. Family squabbles at their worst!

After we discussed her predicament, the manager took a fresh approach. She asked the group to put their rationalizations aside and focus on where they could agree. Persistently, she continued to peel back their layers of differences until they were able to identify a nub of agreement: their shared commitment to the customer. From that point of mutual interest, they went on to resolve the problem, more fully and creatively than they could have imagined.

It is easy to become mired in the *We/They* mindset, and once in it, we tend to cast everything in its shadow. *We* are always the affronted and *they* are always the offenders. Servant Leaders, *Humanagers*, point out when we are lost in the swamp, help us locate a pathway out, restore our common ground, and *re-member* our organizational family. In a healthy organization, *We/They* are always *Us*.

ALL PEOPLE CONNECTED

People are a microcosm of the organization: each of us is in essence a *system*. As individual *systems*, it is not a stretch to say that we have our own internal "executive suite," "finance office," "customer service department," "counseling center," "chaplaincy," "housekeeping and maintenance functions." We are multi-dimensional living systems. A former colleague illustrates it this way[10]:

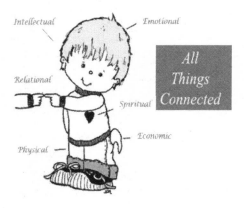

FIGURE 20

We tend to view each other myopically. Leaders can be guilty of compartmentalizing staff, relegating them to the "pigeonhole" in which they were first slotted. If I hire you to manage the Information Technology Department, I see you in the context of your computer capabilities. I may be missing your talent as a violinist or as a deacon in your church. If you were a Nurse Manager when we met, I may not be aware that you have a business degree or are a Colonel in the Reserves. I once inherited an employee whose role was "watchdog," monitoring leaders' compliance with rules and regulations. She was a hard person to get to know, not a soft touch. When I learned that she spent her weekends building Habitat for Humanity homes, I saw her in a different light.

---

10   Thank you, Joan Killinger.

In a personal example, my first after-school job was as an aide in a nursing home. One of my patients, Carrie, had dementia and was a real challenge to care for. She cried constantly, calling out for her deceased husband, wringing her handkerchief, anxious and demanding. I thought of Carrie as a draining assignment. One day I read her patient history and discovered that she had been the organist at a prestigious church in town. I was an organist! My mother had been an organist! At once Carrie became a whole human being instead of merely a dementia patient. Suddenly I had a personal connection with Carrie that I could not ignore. After that, I found myself relating to Carrie with more kindness and patience, and even with joy. We don't always need to know people more deeply; we just need to know them *differently*.

As students training in a hospital, we were admonished to "park our problems at the front door," not to bring *extraneous* issues to work. I have since found that that's impossible. None of the issues of our lives are extraneous. People can't focus on their work if they're worried about paying the mortgage or a family illness or who will watch the kids. In fact, as an employer, I *want* them to bring their full selves to the job. The physician may also be a dynamite writer, the dietician an expert team builder, the secretary a great teacher, and the data clerk a systems thinker. Why would I want to use only one of your dimensions? We are all holistic, multi-dimensional beings. Why would any leader be satisfied with less?

LEADERS ARE PEOPLE, TOO

In VA, when new CREW (Civility, Respect and Engagement in the Workplace) groups are launched, someone invariably asks where the supervisor fits in the scheme. CREW groups are essentially employees who work together on a regular basis, e.g., the radiology staff or the surgical care unit. In CREW, these folks may, for the first time, begin to have honest conversations about tricky issues, with a goal of improving the job climate. Being honest and doing serious interpersonal work among themselves is enough of a challenge, but they often draw the line at doing it with the supervisor in the room.

CREW's response to this conundrum is: supervisors are people too. Supervisors are employees too. They have the same concerns about family, health, performance and career as anyone else. And they are an important part of the team. CREW participants are coached in how to accept the supervisor as a valued member of the group who can help resolve work unit issues. They learn that there is no advantage to excluding the supervisor.

For leaders who are really trying to be *humanagers*, it can be confusing and frustrating when they are seen as the enemy, consigned to the other side of the aisle. One manager told me, "I know I'm a Teddy bear, but to my team, I'm still the boss." As they become more seasoned, leaders understand that in many cases it's the position that keeps staff at arm's length, not the person. Leaders do indeed hold power, but if they are Servant Leaders, they relish sharing that power.

A mentor once advised me, "Your attitude is showing." People watch what leaders say and how they say it, their facial expressions and body language. They try to gauge whether it's a good day to raise an issue with a leader, whether the supervisor has had her morning coffee yet and what kind of mood she's in. And staff will interpret the signs. Leaders need to be transparent and consistent or people will read unintended meaning into the leader's every word, every grimace, every sigh, every nod, and every silence.

"Leaders are people too" is not just a message for staff: it's also a reminder to the leader. It can be overwhelming to consider the degree of responsibility a leader has for the lives of those in his sphere, for decisions that shape the worlds of others and the success of an enterprise. Leaders make mistakes, are sensitive to slights, sometimes simply don't know what to do, never have all the answers, have less authority than people think, are frightened and discouraged and carry emotional wounds into their work relationships: are, in other words, human. *Humanagers,* Servant Leaders, are authentic enough and strong enough to ask for help, admit they don't know, show compassion and mete out mercy.

WHERE THE RUBBER MEETS THE ROAD

 The CEO may be the public face of an organization, the company head who holds the scepter of authority, but in a very practical sense, much of the day-to-day power rests with the first-line supervisor. The role of the supervisor is often underestimated and overlooked. But this indeed is where the rubber meets the road. The supervisor is the narrow point in the organizational hourglass, who determines what sifts through and how fast. What a pivotal role! The supervisor can function either as a channel or a dam, provide traction or friction, and become the senior leader's best line of defense or most impenetrable barrier.

Much research has been done on the impact of first-line managers. We know that employees don't leave their jobs, they leave their supervisors. Data show that the presence of civility in the work area (NCOD, 2013) and the practice of Servant Leadership (Laub, 1991) can dramatically increase employees' satisfaction with their supervisors.

First-line supervisors are often promoted to those positions because they are at the top of their technical career ladder; they are the experts at their specialized competency. In order to advance, they must make the shift into management, and often do so with no real leadership training. I have seen the most proficient physician, the best nurse, the strongest union steward, the most capable accountant struggle when elevated to management circles. The good news is that they bring with them their "models" of supervision. The bad news is that they bring with them their "models" of supervision.

If past experience with supervisors has been negative, the employee is at risk of repeating the very behaviors he detested. He may have been attracted to a supervisory position for the wrong reasons: power *over* others, to redress past wrongs, to obstruct change or to exploit the role for personal gain. In this case, training the candidate for new supervisory responsibilities may or may not be effective in adjusting his temperament and expectations. The proverb, "Hire for attitude; train for skills" is especially wise counsel in selecting supervisors.

All of us have had poor supervisors along the way, and it is certainly possible to claim higher ground, learning from the mistakes of others. But we live what we learn. I believe the best models are the leaders who have shown us how to do it right, who have taught by way of their actions, walked us through tough situations with grace, produced results by creating a values-based environment. I hope we have all experienced those leaders as well.

Candidates who have had affirmative supervisory role models are likely to be attracted for the right reasons: power *with* others, to facilitate change, to impact a broader clientele, to grow more leaders. Here, preparation and coaching can reinforce the attitude and fill the skill gaps.

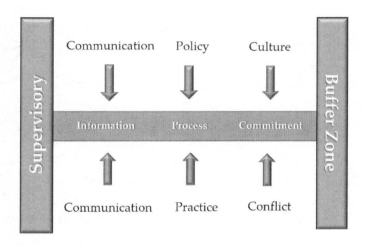

FIGURE 21

Supervisors can be indispensable buffers between the C-Suite and the front line. They field top-down and bottom-up communications and translate them into usable information; they interpret broad policy into processes that result in operative practice; they convert conflict with the corporate culture into commitment.

Supervisors are at the heart of the employee's workday. They reward and recognize, discipline and evaluate; they assign the workload and set expectations. They make the workplace enjoyable, uplifting and fulfilling or demeaning, depressing and depleting. Problems that find their way to the senior leader's office may have been festering with an inept supervisor for ages.

A well-prepared and confident supervisor rarely lets problems get to the executive's desk—not out of fear, but from a sense of accountability, a posture of *primus* with her team and a desire to find solutions closest to the level of the difficulty. The first-line Servant Leader is an extraordinary asset. These are the supervisors who will become ambassadors of *Humanagement*.

A BRIEF NOTE ON THE HUMENVIRONMENT

OK, maybe this is taking the paradigm a bit far, but let's consider for a moment the human aspects of the work environment. Employees don't live in a vacuum. We spend an inordinate amount of time in our work spaces, in conditions that can spark creativity or "dumb us down," spur productivity or dull our senses, isolate us or invite community.

REALITY CHECK ✓

Think about your current work environment: office, cubicle, unit, etc.

- What three factors are most conducive to your work experience?

- What three factors are the most detrimental? Can they be changed?

  Now list the characteristics of your ideal work environment.

Of course work space costs money and must be used prudently, but think about the advantages and disadvantages of:

- Working in cubicles
- Sharing an office
- Open/group space
- "Sick" offices (chemicals, ventilation)
- Assigning square footage by organizational rank
- Hearing multiple conversations simultaneously
- Not being able to hear oneself think
- Lighting and acoustics
- Temperature control
- Distractions
- Privacy and confidentiality
- White noise
- Inadequate team or meeting space
- Break rooms
- Availability of food and refreshment
- Workout rooms or physical activity space
- Resources, technology and virtual connectivity
- Adequate, ergonomic equipment and supplies
- Availability of office/clerical assistance
- Stress-busters and amusement
- Greenery and esthetics

A *Humenvironment* pays dividends in output and efficiency, wellness and innovation, job satisfaction and engagement, teamwork and loyalty. Employees who feel like hamsters on a wheel accomplish about as much.

HUMANAGEMENT AND SERVANT LEADERSHIP

The catchword *'Humanagement'* is essentially a device to capture the attention of leaders at all levels, to underscore the enormity of their influence and impact and to signify the essence of their calling. *Everything the leader says and does leaves a mark.*

Leadership transforms lives. Far from being arrogant, this thought is remarkably humbling. There is no decision, action, strategy or relationship that could not be enriched by mindful contemplation of its human corollary. Servant Leadership envelops and elevates *Humanagement.*

* * *

EMPLOYEE CARE PLAN

Employee's Name:
Supervisor's Name:
Date:

Why did you choose to work in this organization/department/unit?

What will keep you here?

Tell me 3 things that are important to you.

What 3 factors are most important to you/do you enjoy in a job?

What turns you off in a job?

What keeps you up at night?

How would people at your last workplace describe you?

What talents do you have that I might not see at work?

Where would you like to be in 5 years?

What will it take to get there?

How can I help you meet your career goals?

Next Date of Review:

How have we been doing with your career goals?

What else can I do to make your work satisfying?

What would you like to change about your work environment?

FIGURE 22

All Things Connected...

A Veteran customer waiting for service runs out of patience and loses his temper with the Primary Care nurse. Upset, the nurse considers calling Security. Instead, she puts her hand on the Veteran's shoulder and says, "You must feel like you're lost in the system. Let me see what I can do." The nurse could have written off the Veteran. Why didn't she?

A travel clerk notices a patient standing in a long line at the Pharmacy window, looking a bit shaky. The clerk grabs a chair from his office, offers it to the patient and stands with him a few minutes to be sure he's alright. The travel clerk is not responsible for the Pharmacy customer. Why didn't he just let Pharmacy handle it?

An employee makes a grave mistake which could have resulted in harm to a client. The supervisor would be justified in pursuing termination, but the employee shows remorse and insight, and has performed well in the past. The supervisor opts to give her another chance. Why?

A manager has been "losing it" lately—public outbursts, bouts of crying, irritable with staff, missing some critical deadlines. The work unit has become tense and employees are complaining. When they learn that the manager is caring for her dying mother, they decide to offer support. The employees could have lodged a formal grievance or transferred off the unit. Why didn't they?

There is a one-word answer: *compassion*. Compassion is empathy, kindness, benevolence, consideration or caring. It is not just an observation from outside another person's experience, it *enters into that experience with him.* Compassion is the opposite of detachment or indifference. It reflects the capacity and desire to serve.

Compassionate service is also high-quality service. It is the supreme manifestation of customer service. It can't be mandated or policy-driven. The potency of compassion is not that we *have to,* but that we *can.*

We know that transactional work inhibits compassion, that

multi-tasking is the enemy of mindful presence and that technology can be distracting and depersonalizing. What if your job relates more to tasks than to people? Does your customer have to compete for attention with a computer screen? Is your only connection by telephone or email?

Here are some small, but meaningful, opportunities to build compassion into our work:

- Help a caller who's being shuffled from one extension to another

- Give a frazzled colleague a hand

- Forgive someone who has treated you badly

- Offer honest, respectful feedback

- Cut a teammate some slack when she's having a rough day

- Assume the best about a co-worker

- Extend a word of encouragement

- Advocate for a patient/customer, even when it's uncomfortable

- Choose to ignore a slight

- Stand with a colleague who's in trouble

- Be truly happy for someone else's good fortune

Now think back to the opening vignettes. Each potential action would have been justifiable: calling Security, letting Pharmacy take responsibility, firing the employee, reporting the manager. But in each situation, the participants chose to go another way.

By doing so, they achieved different and more desirable outcomes:

- The nurse defused the situation by personally connecting with the Veteran.

- There is no such thing as "He's not my responsibility." The patient received immediate assistance, and the travel clerk modeled serving behavior.

- The supervisor knew this employee would be *exceptionally* careful in the future.

- Staff saw an immediate change in the manager's behavior and built more honest team relationships.

We don't use the term *compassion* very often in business. Some see it as connoting weakness, lack of accountability, letting people off the hook or being soft.

I believe compassion is the ultimate expression of power, in all its altruism, generosity and potential.

Only leaders with courage can be vulnerable enough to show compassion. Only those who accept their own flawed selves can serve imperfect individuals in uncertain situations. Only those comfortable with their own humanity can risk entering into the humanity of others.

...All Things Connected

TOOLBOX ACTIVITY:
Humanagement

❧ Instructions ❧

Humanagers are called upon to make tough decisions and take firm actions. They may have high expectations and hold co-workers accountable, yet they are fair and humane. Even the most arduous leadership responsibilities can be shaped by using a Servant Leader approach.

Think about the situations below. Consider how you could alter the expected outcome by using principles of Servant Leadership or *Humanagement*. Share your answers in a small group.

- Terminating a probationary employee who has not hit the mark
- Informing staff the corporate office is canceling a popular work-at-home policy
- Announcing a new round of budget cuts
- Floating an idea for department consolidation
- Disciplining an employee for bullying
- The department under your supervision did not meet its performance metrics

❧ Discussion ❧

1. How did your answers compare with others in the group?

2. How would a Servant Leader/*Humanager* handle these situations differently?

3. What would the outcomes look like?

4. What untoward effects might be averted?

5. Have you tried this approach in your own work environment? If so, share the experience with the group.

6. Do you agree that leaders can exercise accountability *and* compassion? Explain your response.

TOOLBOX ACTIVITY:
Humanopoly

❧ Instructions ❧

Take a trip around the leadership board. How are you doing?

If you are playing individually, use the game board to review your progress in each of the squares.

If you are in a small group, you can roll dice and proceed, each player talking about their progress on his/her assigned square.

❧ Discussion ❧

1. At which Servant Leader practices do you excel?

2. Where do you recognize opportunities for improvement?

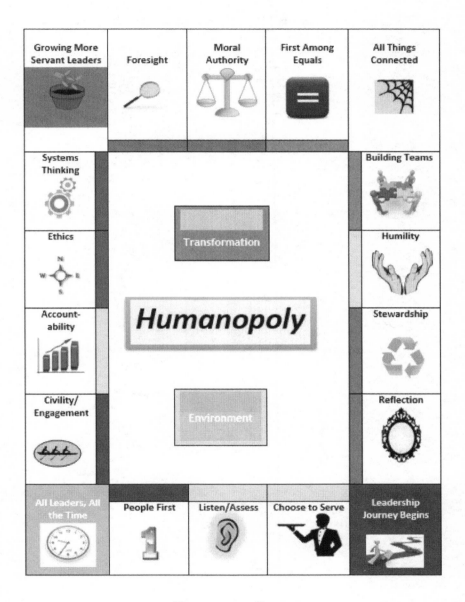

HUMANOPOLY BOARD

ჱ Chapter References ჱ

Greenleaf, R. K. (1970). *The Servant as Leader*. Atlanta, GA: The Greenleaf Center for Servant Leadership.

Laub, J. A. (1999). *Assessing the servant organization: Development of the servant organization leadership assessment instrument*. Dissertation Abstracts International, 60, (02), 308.

Nouwen, H. (1975). *Reaching Out*. New York: Doubleday.

Oshry, B. www.powerandsystems.com. Organization Workshop

Williamson, M. www.inspiringquotes.us

CHAPTER SEVEN

*The Spiritual Side of
Servant Leadership*

All Things Connected...

Organizations are complicated entities. Companies start out with straightforward missions. Before long, they undergo a "cellular mitosis": functions and systems splitting off and multiplying, each concentrating on a different piece of the mission.

Somewhere along the line, one cell goes off track and a program is created to correct the misstep. The organization begins to imagine yet more new programs that can monitor functions and systems and keep them in order.

Some of the programs are beautifully innovative and generate great enthusiasm. As the organizational "cells" proliferate, those programs become increasingly essential to keep them aligned with each other and true to the original mission.

That effort requires oversight. Metrics are established and data are gathered so the organization can prove that the programs are efficient and effective; that all the "cells" are still doing what they set out to do.

I love the way organizations grow and work. I am proud of what many have accomplished. It's exciting to watch the *busyness* and sophistication of their operations.

That said, let me tell you what I really think.

I often envision life as an artichoke or an onion. There is a sweet spot—a simple truth—at the core, yet we spend a lifetime adding layer upon layer of complexity until that truth is obscured. We are misled into thinking that complexity is the normal state. It is not.

I am drawn to the words *agape* (Greek) and *caritas* (Latin) which are so rich with meaning: altruistic love, compassionate love, unconditional love, love of one's fellow man, passionate commitment to the well-being of others.

LOVE IS THE SIMPLE TRUTH AT THE CORE OF COMPLEXITY.

Love is not a word many of us are comfortable using in the workplace. But what if...?

We labor over performance measures, yet if we focused on always doing the right thing, would performance measures be automatically met?

We construct elaborate customer service programs, but if our every action were motivated by agape/caritas, would customer service just happen, would it become the "new normal"? What if the perfect patient experience stemmed from an intrinsic drive to serve, instead of an extrinsic force to compel service?

If our work flowed from love, what kind of relationships would we create? How would we treat each other, our environment? How would we use our resources, human and financial? How accountable would we be for the quality and ethics of our actions?

Would each of us instinctively do the right thing? Would we even need performance standards...or performance appraisals? Policies and procedures? Costly techniques of measurement and safety?

I wonder if the strategies we develop, the systems we build, the checks and balances we accumulate, ultimately serve to distract us from the simplicity of love?

Practically speaking, no one wants to be perceived as naïve or unrealistic. We live and work in a world that demands and generates complexity. That train has left the station.

We may feel the web of complexity holding us ever tighter as we try to extricate ourselves. And so we are tempted to stop struggling....

Yet amid the inevitable complexity, let's not lose sight of that simple truth which, in the last analysis, connects all things.

...All Things Connected

What's love got to do with it…?
—Tina Turner

I f this book were being written a year earlier, this chapter would not
exist. Thirty years in state and federal government have made me
guarded about public discussion of spirituality. Early in my career, I spent
time in Catholic health care systems where many meetings started and
ended with prayer; where groups of staff daily prayed for patients, families and caregivers; where nuns and other religious were in positions of
authority. Although it did not come easily to me, over time I grew to be
fairly comfortable with these public expressions of faith.

Just when I was really starting to appreciate the atmosphere of religious health care, I transitioned to the public sector, an enormous shift
culturally and philosophically. In the leadership positions I held, I had
to be discreet about my beliefs, neutral in conversations about religion,
explicitly ecumenical regarding the religious support of patients.

There were occasions when I felt like I was walking on eggshells to
avoid the subject. An intensely spiritual person by nature, this was not

my authentic self. After a while, I found ways of inserting my spiritual side in innocuous, non-denominational and non-proselytizing ways. For example, I could open a meeting with a reflection or a mindfulness meditation in order to focus the group, set an intention for what we wanted to accomplish and center the participants. Instead of conveying my beliefs in words, I tried all the harder to show them in my actions.

I had taken such efforts to delete overt religious references in my work that when I was asked to facilitate a Servant Leadership retreat for the Sisters of the Sorrowful Mother and their Associates[11], it took some real thought to add it back in! The experience, however, was joyful and liberating. It reinforced for me the importance of honoring our holistic nature.

When making Servant Leadership presentations, I frequently hear two divergent positions:

1. I'm uncomfortable with Servant Leadership because it is a religious concept (or, it conflicts with my religion, or, because I have no religion)

or

2. I'm delighted that Servant Leadership affirms my formal religious beliefs

To both I say, Servant Leadership is neither doctrine nor dogma. It is not religious per se: it is congruent with the tenets of all religions and no religion. The principle of service, of "doing unto others," is found in Christianity, Judaism, Islam, Hinduism, Confucianism and Buddhism, and as a basic tenet of society, in atheism, agnosticism and secular humanism. It is a core premise as well of Carl Jung's collective unconscious (1959), Einstein's theories (Church, 2005), David Hawkins' *Power vs Force* (1995), *A Course in Miracles* (1996) and many others. There is no dearth of sources from which Servant Leaders derive their inspiration.

---

11   Thank you, Diane Wegner.

Regardless of our position on religion, experts point to three spiritual needs common to all of us:

- We need *Love and Relatedness* —to know that we are important not for who or what we are, but ***that*** we are, to understand where we fit into the grander scheme of things and *vis a vis* each other and that each of us is a critical piece of the universal puzzle

- We need *Purpose and Meaning* —purpose links us to the greater context of life around us; meaning assures us that our unique role is worthy, our personal contribution has value

- We need *Forgiveness*—from others for our failings and short-comings, our careless slights and cruelties, for lost opportunities to do good, and from ourselves for not being perfect

Some people express their spirituality in religion, others through art or music, raising children or cultivating a garden, building Habitat homes or being Servant Leaders. It is clear that whether or not we profess a religion, whether or not we are

Everything is either love or a call for love.
– A Course in Miracles

comfortable discussing it, in whatever way we choose to express it, each of us has a spiritual dimension and each of us experiences spiritual needs.

Hints of spirituality are embedded in so many aspects of Servant Leadership: being a person of character and a compassionate collaborator, exercising moral authority, putting others first, using power ethically, nurturing community.

WHAT IS SPIRIT?

Spirit comes from the Latin for *breath*. It is variably described as an animating or life force, soul; an essence or aura; one's inner self; an attitude, mood or outlook; courage, character, determination or vivacity. We use the word in many contexts beyond the religious or metaphysical: team spirit, school spirit, holiday spirit, high spirits, kindred spirits, the spirit of the law, the Spirit of '76. All of these terms imply a sense or ethos which inspires and/or connects. For example, "kindred spirits" connotes something greater than the individuals involved. "Team spirit" represents a transcendent emotion or purpose that connects the members.

Spirit also appears to contain a quality of magnetism, of high resonance that attracts at a sub-conscious level. We all have had the experience of being "pulled" to someone for no apparent reason: maybe their physical appearance or resemblance to someone else, the timbre of their voice or what they are saying, an indefinable *presence*. And each of us has experienced moments when *we* have been the attractors: when we are *in the zone*.

I remember flying to another city to chair an important and, I feared, contentious meeting. While on the plane I began reading a scientific/ spiritual text that I expected would be intellectually challenging to me. To my surprise, I was captivated and felt a startling elevation of spirit, an impression of enveloping peace. I literally walked with lighter steps as I made my way to the office location.

In this glow, I stood outside the doorway to greet participants as they arrived. (This was not my usual practice. I would typically be busy inside, nervously preparing my materials.) As I waited, I noticed that people passing in the hallway seemed drawn to stop and talk; some actually changed course in order to approach me. I became aware that people were moved to reach out and touch me. The participants appeared to brighten as they filed into the meeting.

The day went better than I could have hoped. Collectively, we sensed an atmosphere in the room (revisit Figure 16) that uplifted our group and the work we accomplished together. I do not share this episode lightly or sanctimoniously, but because it was such a singular and magical experience.

SPIRITUAL QUALITIES OF THE SERVANT LEADER

By this point, we should have a clearer idea of the spiritual side of Servant Leadership, are maybe even a bit more comfortable with the concept. There are many spiritual qualities of a Servant Leader, but we'll highlight a few here:

INSPIRATION

Inspire—literally, to breathe in. Traditional leaders can be so busy *doing* that they forget about *being*. Stop for a moment and take a deep breath. That very act triggers your reset button. We exist and function in a world that is complex and chaotic, and becoming more so every day. There is no end in sight, no level ground up ahead where we can stop to rest. We just keep climbing.

Technology evolves at an unrelenting rate, the work world reflects the inexorable march of global events, expectations increase exponentially, we are "on call" in one way or another 24 hours a day, 7 days a week. Thomas Merton (1966) refers to the pace of the modern world as one more small violence to the spirit.

Whether you receive your inspiration from the universe, a walk in the woods or the people around you, your part of the transaction is to accept it. If we are preoccupied with making things happen, we will not recognize inspiration when it arrives. It may show up as the right thought, the best word, a well-timed action, a dazzling opportunity, a flash of wisdom, a revolutionary innovation, the perfect solution. *Inspiration fills us up.*

Servant Leaders are not only inspired, they are inspiring. They generate enthusiasm and create a space for people to "catch the spirit." They applaud the virtuosity and brilliance of others. Because they are less inclined to control or micromanage, Servant Leaders can step back so that others can step forward.

I once wrote a paper on trust. It pointed out how often we trust without really thinking about it. We buy a steak at a restaurant not knowing where it came from or how it was prepared, if it was close to its "use by" date. We board a taxi expecting it to deliver us to our destination safely (despite parental admonitions never to get into a car with a stranger!). We hand the car keys to a teenager or loan our best sweater to a friend or turn over our brightest ideas to a boss. All these are demonstrations of trust.

It's curiously easier to trust the chef and the cab driver whom we don't know and who have no real interest in our welfare, than to trust people with whom we share a personal bond. The explanation is vulnerability. When we trust family and friends, we are putting our emotional well-being in their hands. When we extend that trust to an employer, our financial, professional and intellectual welfare is at stake. A frightening thought, an awesome responsibility.

One of the strongest, most growth-enhancing messages a leader can convey is trust. Several times in my career, I have appointed a "dark horse" candidate to a high-level position and watched them far exceed my expectations. Giving them a chance to lead—sometimes against the odds—was an act of trust that spurred them to success.

Servant Leaders generate trust by demonstrating respect, transparency and consistency. Some examples:

- Applying rules impartially
- Meting out discipline uniformly
- Communicating fully and honestly
- Using the "no surprises" rule: employees should always know where they stand
- Giving timely and constructive feedback
- Delegating responsibility
- Involving staff in a change
- Demonstrating ethical behavior
- Sharing credit liberally
- Ensuring a psychologically safe environment

Trust is a tricky concept: while its presence is important, the lack of it often speaks more loudly. I recall a situation where a street sign on the grounds of a Medical Center had been defaced. Because it was located on the outskirts of the property, the Director had not noticed it, but someone did, and contacted the Director's corporate boss in another city. The Director completed the repairs and phoned Corporate to assure them it had been remedied. An hour later, the boss' secretary called to demand a photo of the sign to confirm the repairs. That request for evidence conveyed a disheartening lack of trust to Medical Center staff: that their integrity was questioned and that the assurance of their CEO was not good enough.

Delegating a task then monitoring every step does not communicate trust. Claiming credit for an employee's suggestions does not encourage further innovation. Assuming the worst about a team member before gathering the facts does not cultivate a trusting environment. Over-promising and under-delivering keeps people off-balance. Micromanagement in itself is a clear message of distrust, and a potent dissatisfier.

Exercising trust does not make us doormats, and trust is not an abdication of accountability. There is wisdom in the adage, "Trust, but verify," although I have seen that phrase used to justify a "gotcha" style of management. In certain situations trust must be earned and in others it is simply owed. The Servant Leader does not exploit that trust or take it for granted.

I love the example of the company that was experiencing an intolerable loss of office supplies through employee theft. A package of pencils here, Post-it Notes there, tape, paper, paperclips, etc., seemed to walk out the door in small enough amounts that staff was unfazed by the pilfering. The company considered options like hiring security or checking employees' bags as they punched out but was concerned about relaying just the right message. In the end, they installed a supply cupboard next to the time clock, filled it with office items people used at home and invited staff to help themselves judiciously. The solution cost the company little and the illicit appropriation of supplies ceased. Employees gained a sense of responsibility for their actions; they felt respected and trusted to hold up their end of the arrangement.

Trust is a two-way street: it is reciprocal. We owe each other the responsibility and reverence of trust. Leaders who hold the work relationship *in trust* display stewardship and exemplify the Golden Rule. In Servant Leadership, trust is a grace bestowed.

MERCY

In some ways, this is a tough one. Leaders can get fidgety about the concept of mercy: what about justice? Does mercy make me a dupe? Will employees take advantage of me? Will my boss lose respect for me?

It's interesting that the notion of being seen as a doormat surfaces repeatedly. I wonder why we are so worried about being thought of as servants, as trusting or as merciful. Is there something upside-down about that thinking?

Mercy is shown when:

- A stressed colleague's angry outburst is overlooked

- An employee who "falls off the wagon" is offered a last-chance agreement

- An alternative to termination is sought for an honest mistake

- The spirit of the policy matters more than its letter

- A deadline is extended for a team member suffering a family crisis

> *The quality of mercy is not strained. It droppeth as the gentle rain from heaven upon the place beneath: it is twice blest; it blesseth him that gives and him that takes.*
>
> – William Shakespeare

Mercy is not without consequence: it travels with accountability. It often requires some form of atonement: amends, apologies or reparation.

Nothing in this book—or anywhere in the Servant Leadership literature—suggests that poor performance or bad behavior should be disregarded.

Here again, Servant Leadership is countercultural. When the work world cuts employees no slack, the Servant Leader seeks the benefit of the doubt. While traditional leadership urges swift and strict justice, the Servant Leader strives to temper justice with mercy. When the organization shows contempt, the Servant Leader shows compassion.

Mercy is strength.

And here's another subversive thought: mercy is never earned, it is freely given.

STEWARDSHIP

Accountability is a term every leader understands, but there is less familiarity with its first cousin, stewardship. Accountability as a management virtue has been sullied in recent times as societal institutions have turned it into a pejorative, demanding censure and a culprit. Accountability is more apt to be perceived as externally motivated, often out of fear.

In one organization, managers were called upon to "certify" that they had done selected job duties, such as documenting that safety checks were made, that data were accurate or that staff were complying with a policy. To make those certifications, managers had to rely on the honesty and good will of departmental experts and front-line employees. Guarantees of this nature are often simply a "cover" for the next management level, shielding them from blame if something goes wrong, and a "catch" for the certifying supervisor who is left out on a limb if a failure occurs. Accountability now carries a flush of shame.

Stewardship is a bit more ambiguous and nuanced than accountability, but carries none of the baggage. Even leaders who aren't fully clear on its meaning understand that stewardship is a good thing and reflects on them positively. Stewardship is deeper than accountability, reflecting an intrinsic motivation rooted in one's beliefs. It suggests obligations of protection and guardianship, careful and responsible management of something entrusted to one's care. It signifies more than mere safekeeping, but also shepherding to increase the return, as in leaving the workplace better than one found it.

Leaders are stewards of the organization's human and financial resources, its time, materials, work environment and reputation and (in deference to the key practice of Foresight) its future. The leader does not own any of those assets, only makes use of them, regarding them as "on loan" and under his/her aegis for the highest purposes of the organization.

THE POWER OF BELIEF

Men and women don't choose Servant Leader lives for the fun of it, or because there is no easier way to live, but because of their professed beliefs. They don't practice mercy and stewardship for the *quid pro quo*, but because mercy and stewardship are in alignment with their value system.

While they may be extraordinarily varied, a set of beliefs is espoused by each of us that, consciously or unconsciously, guides our actions. We may not even be aware of our beliefs until they are challenged or until we are compelled by circumstances to examine them, but the results can be momentous. Our core beliefs inevitably direct us to the job, the spouse, the profession and the causes that are in synchrony with who we are.

The LeaderServe program (Magellan, 2005) and others use an exercise to illustrate the impact of beliefs on an organization's culture, strategies and ultimate outcomes. I have adapted that premise to incorporate *root cause analysis,* the technique of digging deeper into a situation to find its unseen origins.

Here is an example:
- o The event: amidst highly unflattering media coverage, a product on the market is recalled due to safety concerns.
    - o Sometime prior to the event, a management decision was made to construct the product with cheaper materials. That decision directly or indirectly led to the event.
        - o The choice to cut corners reflected the company's culture of maximizing profit by moderating quality.

o The culture was built on the organizational belief that customers care more about price than quality, and that the benefits of this corporate strategy outweighed the risks.

   o However, the beliefs of individual employees were offended by this philosophy, leading to sabotage and whistleblower complaints.

In the image in Figure 23, the publicized event is represented by the leaves on the tree; the decisions are the branches from which the leaves sprout; the culture is the tree trunk supporting the whole structure; the group/individual beliefs are the roots.

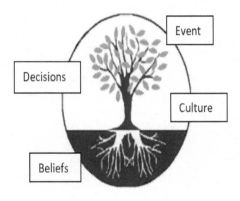

FIGURE 23

Every situation—positive or negative—is the culmination of the leader's strategy, vision and expected outcomes; the organization's culture or historical patterns and the deeply held beliefs that drive behavior. *Behavior is based on belief.* (There are, of course, some beliefs systems that should not see the light of day, e.g., those that reflect prejudice or hatred. We will not address those here.) "The event" is the catalyst that spurs us to action and upon which we base our next steps. But if we only focus on the event itself, we miss the layers of underlying causes, thus often compounding our mistakes.

In order to understand this model more practically, try "working it backwards": from the event to the decision/strategy, through the culture, and finally to the operant beliefs. Try to expose the roots of the crisis by asking the following questions:

- What was the initial problem for which a strategy was created?
- What leadership strategy triggered the event?
- Could alternate strategies have been attempted?
- What cultural dynamics played into the event?
- What group or individual beliefs may have been offended?
- If the intensity of the beliefs had been taken into account, could the outcome have been different?

Let's look at another situation, a health care example this time, then "work it backwards" by subjecting it to the questions above.

The new President of the Elmgrove General Hospital in rural Montana has been scorched by local media and community leaders for supplementing the permanent medical staff with contract service personnel and temporary doctors. The quality of patient care is dramatically declining.

What was the initial problem for which the strategy was created?
A shortage of qualified physicians

What leadership strategy triggered the event?
The decision to contract out medical care

Could alternate strategies have been attempted?
Yes: more aggressive recruitment strategies that would entice doctors to relocate to the area and become part of the community. This option could be less expensive than contract costs

What cultural dynamics played into the event?
In the spirit of many small communities, the culture here is fiercely independent, heritage-proud and historically wary of newcomers; families are intergenerational

What group or individual beliefs may have been offended?
Beliefs about autonomy, supporting local resources, an aversion to "importing" providers who are not committed to the hospital, concerns about the qualifications of temporary staff, impracticality of establishing long-term relationships with contract physicians, a custom of revering doctors as pillars of the community. "We can take care of this ourselves!"

If the intensity of the beliefs had been taken into account, could the outcome have been different?
Yes. The new President himself was unfamiliar with and not yet trusted by the community. If he had better understood the community's beliefs, perhaps a compromise might have been reached. He could have found common ground (we all want high-quality care; we do not have enough physicians to provide it); and acceptable solutions (we will advertise an attractive recruitment package, and use contract staff only until we reach 50% of our recruitment goal). Such an outcome would have built trust and goodwill, garnered community support, enhanced the quality of care and reputation of the hospital and honored local culture and beliefs

In a learning organization, "working it backwards" will inform how such a situation can be handled better *next time*.

REALITY CHECK ✓

Can you think of a situation or event in your workplace
that didn't go as planned? Try to "work it backwards."
What impact could beliefs have had on the outcome?

Why have we spent so much time talking about beliefs? Beliefs are the submerged pilings that shore up the harbor. Visible or not, they undergird the work. Someone once said, "Beware the danger of an unrecognized belief." A leader can dismiss or quash those beliefs for a time, but they eventually bubble up and declare themselves. Staff cannot function in a state of "values dissonance" for long without hurting themselves or the workplace.

Any beliefs, deeply held, are spiritual in that they lay bare our souls, go to the heart of who we are. When our beliefs are threatened, so is our very being. The brilliance of beliefs is that if they can sabotage the system, they can also make it sing! Employees whose higher beliefs are harmonious with the organization's culture and values, and are welcomed and encouraged, become co-creators of the organization. Servant Leaders are optimists about beliefs. If the roots, the trunk and the branches are in alignment, they will bear strong, beautiful and healthy leaves. Marshaling the fervent beliefs of service-driven employees is powerful indeed.

But what if our beliefs are hopelessly incompatible?

There are two realms of supposition about this. Some thought-leaders exhort us to remain where it is challenging to stay, and work from within to change the environment. Joan Chittister (2004) talks about the very act of "grappling" to quit, and of finding ourselves "wherever we are." She advises that we don't change our circumstances, we change our attitudes. Conversely, Matthew 10:14 counsels that "If anyone will not welcome you or hear your words, leave and shake the dust off your feet."

I must admit that I have presented to a few audiences that were so inhospitable to the idea of Servant Leadership, I counted the minutes until I could shake the dust off my feet! We all have moments like that, but for one caught in an untenable work situation, the conflict can be intolerable.

Take Elizabeth, who faced a demoralizing work experience for several years. When she summoned the courage to switch jobs, she deliberately searched for an employer who practiced Servant Leadership. She found a help-wanted notice on the website of a company that billed itself as a Servant Leader organization. Her online research and interviews with the prospective boss convinced Elizabeth that this would be a good match. She was enthusiastic about her involvement in a local Servant Leadership group and anxious to be immersed in that kind of environment.

It did not take long to realize that the facility did not practice what it preached. Although the parent corporation and governing bodies adhered to the philosophy, the new CEO had no concept of Servant Leadership and created a pervasive toxic environment. For months, Elizabeth tried to work from within the organization to nudge changes along, becoming progressively more discouraged. When she finally had to accept that the CEO was not responsive, and saw her health deteriorating as a consequence, Elizabeth "shook the dust off her feet."

I subscribe to the "change from within" ideology as a rule, being convinced that no genuine change occurs *except* from within. **And**, I affirm that in the exceptional cases where doors and minds are irrevocably closed, walking away may be the wisest and kindest course of action.

MEA CULPA

It is in contemplating stories like the one above that Servant Leaders remember the times when we failed: what we've done that we shouldn't have; what we neglected to do that we could have done; when our ignorance, thoughtlessness, lack of moral courage or the weightiness of our decisions have caused people harm.

I know their names; I see their faces. My failures haunt me.

This is the moment when Servant Leaders must humbly acknowledge the universal spiritual need of forgiveness, hope those they have hurt can forgive them and try to forgive themselves.

REALITY CHECK ✓

Take some time to consider those who may have been adversely impacted by your actions. Think of their names or picture their faces. Do you look back and say, "I can't believe I did that!"?

- Were you able to, or can you now, make amends?
- Have they helped you grow as a leader?

SPIRITUAL SELF-HELP FOR SERVANT LEADERS: WITHDRAWAL & REFLECTION

The hectic pace of work offers us little opportunity for meditative musing, but without that, we can never get off the merry-go-round. Periodically we need to be "onlookers from the balcony," where we step outside the leader role and observe—in a non-judgmental way—what we have been doing and how we've been doing it.

One aspect of withdrawal is *disconnecting*: from the smartphone, the texting, and the incessant social media. For many, this requires real self-discipline. It may also involve saying "no" to bosses and colleagues who don't understand the meaning of personal time, who expect leaders to be perpetually on-call.

The ability to withdraw is a vital characteristic that allows Servant Leaders to refresh, reorient and recharge, if only for a moment. I view withdrawal almost as the flip side of foresight: it enables us to look inward in order to look forward.

To withdraw and reflect casts us in the image of modern day *women at the well*, regularly replenishing our own spirits so we have something to give to others. We can't give what we don't have.

If you need a "quantifying" argument, there is actually a business case, which asserts that leaders who engage in reflection are better able to:

- Gain perspective
- Absorb complex information
- Use intuition
- Produce creative thoughts and ideas
- Defuse emotionally charged situations
- Make wiser decisions
- Plug into a greater consciousness

That reflective space is where the hidden mechanisms of leadership take place: the internal workings that imperceptibly connect the moving parts of the organization, the unseen schematics that choreograph the movements.

Reflection is where the struggles are brought to peace, and the obscurities are brought to light.

The functions of withdrawal and reflection are performed in spiritual stillness.

Trying to teach executives about reflection is excruciating! These leaders are action-oriented, not introspective, and often regard it as *fluff*. Even when the business case is persuasive, reflection is still viewed as unrealistic. I have heard all the excuses, most of which revolve around time: I have no time to sit and daydream; I already put in 12-hour days; when I try to sneak in some quiet time, there's always someone wanting "just a few minutes;" if I'm not getting something done I'm wasting time.

If time is your issue, *manage it*! One executive meditates on his lunch breaks, another puts a Do Not Disturb sign on her door for 15 minutes at the end of the day, another reflects to soothing music on the train ride home. Opportunities for reflection won't magically appear: they must be carved out of the workday. Once a regular time and place for reflection is established, it should be inviolable. There are too many pretexts for interrupting or postponing reflection, most of them bogus.

Using time as an excuse may, in fact, be a defense mechanism. The rumination, reassessment, *mea culpas* and self-examination of reflection is uncomfortable work. It is no surprise that many of us would rather be preparing a budget or managing a crisis than exploring our inner depths.

WORK AS A SPIRITUAL BATTLEFIELD

Despite my tenure in VHA, I am not given to war analogies. Yet many of us experience the work as a battleground where struggles are replayed every day: struggles for authority and power, for recognition and voice, for principle and the highest good. Generosity confronts greed, justice disputes with mercy, service campaigns against control, and stewardship clashes with self-interest. Work is the ground on which these nobler battles are fought.

> *In my view of the world there are people whom I would call "spirit carriers." Servants who nurture the human spirit are spirit carriers. They serve to connect those who do the work of the world. Those servants find the resources and make the intensive effort to be an effective influence. They are spirit carriers; they connect the prophecy with the people so that it changes their lives.*
>
> – Robert K. Greenleaf

Servant Leaders rightfully see their work as a vocation, a mission, a ministry, a crusade; a calling to right the collective wrongs; an opportunity to do ordinary things with extraordinary love. The workplace is a community of spiritual beings. Work is connected to everything else, and, in its resonance with the universe, is sacred.

216

All Things Connected...

When I recall the times that felt best in my life, I think of my wedding, my children's births, deep sharing with a friend, the soul-fullness of a walk in the woods, playing a pipe organ, the heartfelt respect of colleagues. Each of these was an instance of *connection*.

My worst memories have to do with family arguments, feeling ignored or rejected, losing a loved one—times of profound disconnection and separation.

We've seen the stunning consequences of disconnectedness splashed across our nightly news, events that shock and cause us to wonder how things have gotten to such a point. But the seeds of separation are quietly sown every day, and *we are complicit*—when we marginalize different viewpoints, villainize a political party or religious belief, commit careless acts of wounding or retaliation, are judgmental or make negative assumptions, fail to listen, display cynicism, mistrust and carry "we/they" attitudes: *anything that excludes, shuts out and cuts off.*

Our society promotes a culture of separation. We work in "silos." We take great pains—as individuals, teams and organizations—to broadcast our uniqueness, what sets us apart, how we are better than others. In our quest for a competitive edge, the human element can easily be overlooked.

Well-meaning people get caught up in doling out and deflecting zingers and gotchas. We become casualties of accountability, constructive criticism and the pace of change. Over time we acquire a self-protective membrane to help us absorb and tolerate all the small violences. We begin to regard the world as a fearful place, and we put up walls to distance ourselves from it and each other.

We need to call a global *time out*, create a sacred space, where we can shed the layers of doubt and defensiveness that accumulate and shield us from the incessant little hurts and violations of the spirit, a moment when "business as usual" becomes "peace on earth," a time in which we can do more than put our differences aside, we can transcend them.

Quantum physics tells us that perception is a mirror: *what we look upon is our state of mind reflected outward,* and that *separation is an illusion.* Our fondest recollections and greatest accomplishments are born in connection.

The events and terrors of this world should press us to contemplate what is really meaningful in life, which, for me, can be understood in three words: *gratitude, compassion and peace.*

Gratitude...

- For recognizing the value of family, friends and faith
- For opportunities to bring light, love and unity; to heal bodies minds and relationships
- For lessons gently learned
- For work that is vocation and not just a job, and the colleagues that make it so
- For what comforts, chafes and challenges us on our journey

Compassion...

- Not "feeling sorry for" or "finding excuses for," but "entering into with"

- It's the difference between judging someone and walking in their shoes. How do we enter into a person's pain, anger or fear, homelessness, isolation or vulnerability?
- And if compassion is not just a mental exercise, what action do we then take?

We should resolve never to let policy, prejudice or public opinion get in the way of practicing compassion. *Practice makes perfect.*

Peace...

Mother Teresa of Calcutta was known for doing ordinary things with extraordinary love. We who are in health care, we who are leaders, engage in actions that are sometimes heroic, although most of what we do each day seems so ordinary and routine.

We forget that doing small things with great love raises them to the level of heroism.

My deepest wish for each of us is that...

We experience gratitude,

We practice compassion,

We live peace.

...All Things Connected

TOOLBOX ACTIVITY:
Valuing Others

❧ Instructions ❧

The Sanskrit word, *Namaste*, conveys the message, "The highest in me honors the highest in you." It is easy to get caught up in the frantic tempo of the day and so miss opportunities to honor or appreciate the people who touch our lives. Take a moment to do that now.

In the grid below, list as many individuals as you can in 10 minutes. Include work colleagues, friends and family members. Then write a word or two that describes what you value most about them, why they are important or what they add to your life.

Name	How do they add value?

Sometime during the next week, try to touch base with the individuals you named and tell them why you value them. If you find this part of the activity difficult, stretch beyond your comfort zone. You may be surprised at how mutually gratifying and beneficial the effort can be.

≈ Discussion ≈

1. Think beyond the assigned roles or responsibilities of the names above. Could you be guilty of pigeonholing them? Might they have additional skills and talents that you are missing?

2. How often do you stop to consider the value of individuals in your workgroup?

3. When was the last time you expressed gratitude or showed appreciation to someone for all the gifts they bring to the table?

4. In what concrete ways can you structure appreciation into your day?

5. When you shared with the people on your list why you value them, how did they respond?

REFLECTION

Think honestly about:

What prevents me from regular reflection?

What *specifically* can I do to ensure time for reflection?

Time:

Place:

Other considerations:

❧ Chapter References ❧

Chittister, J. (2004). *Called to Question: A Spiritual Memoir*. Lanham, MD: Sheed and Ward.

Church D. (2005). *Einstein's Business: Engaging Soul, Imagination and Excellence in the Workplace*. Santa Rosa, CA: www.EliteBooksOnline.com

Foundation for Inner Peace. (1996). *A Course in Miracles*. New York: Viking Penguin.

Frick, D. (2013). "Lessons You Can Use from the Life of Robert K. Greenleaf." Presented at the International Conference on Servant Leadership. Indianapolis, IN.

Hawkins, D. R. (1995). *Power vs Force*. USA: Hay House.

Jung, C. (1959). *The Archetypes and the Collective Unconscious*. Princeton, NJ: Princeton University Press.

Keith, K. M. (2015). *The Christian Leader at Work*. Honolulu, HI: Terrace Press.

LeaderServe Workshop. (2005). *Magellan Executive Resources*, Minneapolis, MN.

Merton, T. (1966). *Conjectures of a Guilty Bystander*. New York: Doubleday.

Shakespeare, W. (1596). *The Merchant of Venice*. Act IV, Scene 1. www.poets.org.

www.usccb.org/bible/matthew/10

CHAPTER EIGHT

All Leaders, All the Time

All Things Connected...

Every season of the year presents a stimulus for reflection: the new beginnings of spring, summer break, getting back into the routines of fall and the quiet turning inward of winter.

Whichever suits you best, choose a time to recharge, recommit and reconnect. We need to attend to our own wellness, equilibrium and inner peace in order to be effective leaders, co-workers and caregivers. And make no mistake, all of us—not just those in health care professions—are caregivers.

I call this "the fine line between drowning and walking on water."

We're all subject to personal, professional and societal stressors. We juggle many roles: dedicated employee, devoted spouse/parent/child, student and volunteer, church and club member. We're conditioned to expect superhuman performance of ourselves and everyone around us, and we feel let down when those expectations aren't met.

Conflict between competing demands requires us to find some stability—where we can go with the flow, keep our heads above the surface, even when we're swimming against the current.

Wellness is harmony among all our dimensions. It's the wholeness of holistic health. We are physical, emotional, intellectual, spiritual and relational beings. The workplace is enriched by our multi-dimensional presence.

I want nothing less than *all* the gifts you bring.

Each dimension is inextricably linked and we cannot neatly separate them, although there is often pressure to do so:

It's difficult to enjoy a social event when you're anxious about bills

You can't park a family crisis at the door, even though we're told it's unprofessional to bring problems to work

Performance is bound to suffer if we can't get along with co-workers

It's hard to be engaged in a workplace whose values conflict with yours

It's tough to maintain a "service first" mentality when you're worried about the latest round of budget cuts

Vacation is unlikely to be a time of renewal if the smartphone is always on

The *fine line* is decidedly personal. In my journey, I've found a few guideposts to help me stay on course. Maybe some of them will help you as well.

ASSERTIVENESS: not to be confused with aggressiveness! Holding to my "true north" while respecting the rights of others. Practicing honesty, integrity, authenticity and trust. Being able to say "No" while delighting in saying "Yes." For me (and for most introverts), *every day* is an exercise in assertiveness.

SYSTEMS THINKING: accepting that everything is connected to everything else. Nothing I do or think or say is in a vacuum, will not affect something or someone, somewhere (the Butterfly Effect).

There are three choices for **CONFLICT RESOLUTION:** *fight, flight or look at it in a different light.* Quantum physics demonstrates that we see things the way we expect to see them. How we handle conflict is truly our choice.

Instead of lamenting what was left undone today, **CONGRATULATE YOURSELF** for what was. Develop an aptitude for joy!

SUPPORT RATHER THAN COMPETE: do I build people up or tear them down? Forge partnerships or sabotage them? Most of us operate from a scarcity mindset: if someone gains, someone has to lose. Budgets may work that way, but the universe doesn't.

PRIORITIZE family, personal and professional obligations carefully. We may not have the luxury of a 40-hour week, but workaholism is just another *cheap thrill*.

VIEW THINGS FROM AN ON LOAN PERSPECTIVE: I'm a steward of my work, my home, my family and my resources. They are mine for a while, to take care of and make the most of. If I use all my energy trying to hold on to things, I'll have none left to enjoy them.

REAL POWER has little to do with position, status or control. Power is the capacity generated by relationships.

Without a spiritual **GROUNDING**, the next wave will knock us off balance. While the circumstances of our lives may change, the values and ethics within which we operate do not.

YOUR ATTITUDE IS SHOWING!

We teach others continuously about accountability, service, kindness, and balance—not by what we say and do, but by *who we are* and how others *experience* us.

We are people in service to others. We ceaselessly give of ourselves, but we cannot give what we do not have.

The choice is *not* between drowning and walking on water: we can elect instead to be whole, healthy, balanced human beings. We are each in charge of our own journey.

Holistically healthy individuals produce healthy organizations.

Walking on water is an abnormal state.

...All Things Connected

You gotta make your own kind of music...
—The Mamas and the Papas

N o one can tell us how to "show up" as a Servant Leader. We write
our own lyrics and compose our own score. We follow the same
principles, but the finished composition is unique.

There are illustrations of service all around us. We need good servants. But not all servants are leaders and not all service is leadership
(Keith, 2012). Is everyone who leads a Servant Leader? No, many leaders
fall short on the list of characteristics and practices that define the organizational Servant Leader. But Servant Leadership has never required one
to hold a formal leadership position. People in official leadership roles
also lead outside of work. People not in official leadership roles find legitimate ways to lead at work and in their communities. Everyone in the
workplace is encouraged to be a Servant Leader. I have deeply considered
the paradoxes and have come to appreciate that anyone who *serves first*
and *who goes out ahead to show the way in that service* is a Servant Leader.

To me, "***We are all leaders, all the time,***" is an aspirational statement. We may fail repeatedly, and in many aspects of life, but we are
called to serve by leading nonetheless. I continue to believe that none of
us gets a pass. The world cannot afford to allow any of us to watch from
the wings. While we may not all be leaders in the classical sense, it's time

for everyone to claim their niche for service, to stand up and show the way. Greenleaf said, "What matters is what we do in our little corner of the world, and why we are doing it" (Frick, 2004).

"Why we are doing it" is the operant phrase. Sometimes the small services we perform seem so trivial that we fail to equate them with Servant Leadership. Is every good deed Servant Leadership? Clearly not. Good deeds can be done out of selfish motives: not Servant Leadership, but still good deeds. In my estimation, every act of service offered from the instinct or intent to *serve first* can reflect Servant Leadership. Every work of public service, charity and volunteerism is elevated when it arises from an inner desire to serve.

Leadership is "stepping up." "Stepping up" is a personal decision to serve. We don't need to wait for permission to step up: we often do it without thinking. It becomes who we are. I have been touched by people who would never call themselves Servant Leaders. Whatever their walk of life, they have distinguished themselves in at least one Servant Leader behavior or trait. Few of us can claim we have "arrived," but many have "stepped up," led by showing and doing, modeled a quality of service that inspires others to serve.

Throughout this chapter I will recognize some of those muses in my own life, sharing one instance of how they manifest as Servant Leaders. They might encourage you on your Servant Leader journey. Here are the first:

> **Alex** ... for listening that heals
> **Denise** ... who gives everyone a sense of possibility
> **Donna** ... for her generosity of time and trust
> **Raphael** ... who empowered lay people to become spiritual leaders
> **Dorothy** ... for leading others to love through music
> **Kelly** ... who took risks in finding common ground
> **Rhonda** ... for "stepping up" through a friend's illness

We are so accustomed to noticing the opposite that it is startling how many examples of service we see once the level of awareness is fine-tuned. I dedicated one day not long ago to observing and identifying Servant Leader behaviors, and this is what I found:

- A customer giving up her place in the grocery line
- A woman picking up the contents of a stranger's spilled purse
- A clerk adding her own money when a shopper was short
- A colleague interrupting her own work to help a team member
- A teenager opening the door for an overburdened package delivery man
- A co-worker organizing an office food drive for a local charity
- A church member with a debilitating disease offering to facilitate a family support group
- A woman driving her elderly neighbor to the senior center
- A postal worker patiently helping a confused patron
- An employee standing up for a colleague who was being mistreated
- A man stopping to give money to a homeless Veteran AND connecting him with the VA Medical Center for care
- A friend sending birthday cards to shut-ins

I may have missed a few, but the list is fairly impressive: small and not so small actions that sent the message of Servant Leadership. We have no way of reading what was in the hearts of these people, but I would posit that their acts of service were not haphazard, rather demonstrations of a thoughtful philosophy of serving, of deliberately "stepping up" to show the way.

~~~~~~

REALITY CHECK ✓

Pick a day and watch for evidence of Servant Leadership.
How many instances did you find? Did you identify missed
opportunities for service? What did you learn from this exercise?

~~~~~~

THINKING BIG

Even if our Servant Leader actions are small, our Servant Leader thinking can be big. Unless we are in positions of power, we question our ability to be influential. Figure 24 illustrates the spheres within which we can influence.

PERSONAL influence allows us to make an impact, one act of service at a time: helping a team member, throwing change into Santa's kettle, donating clothing. *Influencing at the point of service.*

PROFESSIONAL influence expands our impact to the workplace, institutionalizing Servant Leader practices and creating structures that support them: a CREW initiative, corporate charities and customer service programs. *Influencing at the point of organizational performance.*

SOCIAL influence extends our impact to the community and beyond: ensuring healthy populations, supporting legislation, advocacy of the marginalized, joining a political campaign. *Influencing at the point of public policy.*

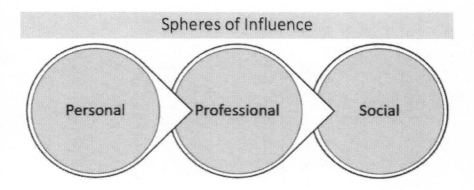

FIGURE 24

A line from the Eagles song, "Desperado," reads, "Come down from your fences; open the gate." Yes, it is safer to deny our call to lead and influence than to risk failure. Sitting astride the fence and behind the gate keeps us neutral, out of the line of fire. Regrettably, we do not ask too much of ourselves: we ask far too little. On the next few pages we'll explore some of the chief reasons why.

LEARNING AT THE SPEED OF LIGHT

In many situations, people have learned *not* to be leaders. They may see leading as "above their pay grade;" they may have tried to lead in the past with unsatisfactory results. From learning theory we know that thoughts like these can pattern themselves over time and produce conditioned responses. These "programmed tapes" click on automatically in our heads when a familiar stimulus occurs. You might be familiar with these:

- Workers learn to avoid the boss until she's had her morning coffee

- When a child is teased for getting good grades, he learns to "dumb down" his work

- If employees' suggestions are routinely ignored, they learn to quit making them

- When one spouse is overly critical, the other one learns to be defensive

- A manager learns to avoid a chronic complainer

Because a leader is anyone willing to help, we can celebrate the fact that the world is abundantly rich in leaders. Some people ask, "Where have all the leaders gone?" But if we worry that there's a shortage of leaders, we're just looking in the wrong place, usually at the top of some hierarchy. Instead, we need to look around us. And we need to look at ourselves.

– Margaret Wheatley

- When work processes are too demanding or don't make sense, we learn to "game the system"

- When staff see punitive results, they learn not to take risks or tell difficult truths

Programmed tapes guide many of our responses. They kick in unconsciously, and that is exactly the problem. They allow other people, previous interactions and history to determine how we react. This condemns us to repeating past behaviors and stifles growth. We can choose our responses and behaviors based on the present. Do you want to "step up" as a leader *now?* Are you ready to chance a new direction? Are you prepared to think differently?

A number of years ago, a graduate RN who had been working in my department for several months came to my office crying at the end of her shift. "I want to resign," she sobbed. "I'm inadequate as a nurse. I'm not completing my assignments. Today I was late passing medications, I skipped a dressing change and I didn't have time to do my diabetic teaching. By any standard, I failed." "So what did you accomplish today?" I asked. She replied, "All I was able to do was to sit with Mr. Paul while he died."

This nurse "stopped the line." She put aside the tasks of time to meet the demands of relationship, but her "programmed tapes" drowned out the sweet music of her *mitzvah*.

We are constantly learning: we are constantly teaching. Sometimes we need to throw away the old programmed tapes that hold us back, that instill guilt, to *unlearn* patterns that have outlived their usefulness. In this context, what should you *unlearn* today?

Marc ... an advocate for the powerless and disenfranchised
Leketha ... for her quiet courage and humility
Harriet ... in her service to aging parents
Linda ... who has always put others' needs before her own
Fr. Terry ... for his compassion, charity, and conviction
Kasey ... for her loving patience
Stan ... for bringing a tradition of caring leadership into retirement

---

TRANSITION AND CHANGE

Accepting the mantle of leadership indicates a new level of maturity, and it is not achieved overnight. Transition is a fact of life. It's a process. We transition from childhood to adulthood, civilian to military and to Veteran, single to married and perhaps to parenthood, employment to retirement, life to death. Transitions are often difficult, bittersweet. There is always a coming from and a going to, giving up one existence and embracing another.

Transition is the interstitial space between a known state and an unknown state. Transition can be hard because it signals change. But for aspiring Servant Leaders, it can be a time of possibility, of unfolding, when we stop clutching what has been and become curious about what can be.

Most of us imagine that external forces are directing transition and change, and that we are pawns of fate. We think that the universe is shaping us—that we have little power and significance. The study of biocentrism (Lanza, 2009) tells us the reverse: that our collective consciousness is shaping the world around us as we read this.

If we believe something is true, we must act differently. If we understand that all thoughts create form on some level, we must think differently. If we recognize the repercussions of our words, we must speak more carefully. If we wish to create a unified environment, we must behave in ways that are unifying. If we comprehend that our decisions affect those around us, we must lead in ways that elevate our workplace. *We cannot profess a truth and fail to be changed by it.*

Dr. Ed, PhD, was one of several lay members of the governing board of a Catholic health care system. Up until that moment, the term "system" could be used loosely. But at this board meeting, the Sisters, community leaders and business executives present were preparing to ratify an agreement that would merge the loose confederation of hospitals into a legitimate corporation, which included a shared distribution of resources.

Preach the gospel at all times. When necessary, use words.

– St. Francis of Assisi

The board wrangled for hours about what the budget of the respective hospitals should be. "St. Joe's ought to be self-sufficient", "St. Rose shouldn't have to carry Sacred Heart," "All Souls will be a drain on St. Mary's." Every representative argued forcefully for their "fair share" of the budget. When the tension was reaching its peak, Dr. Ed quietly raised his hand and said, "Are we not our brother's keeper?"

You are a change agent. It's part of your job description and mine, whatever that job is. Managing change in consonance with our values, with enthusiasm, wisdom, generosity and grace, is simply part of our pilgrimage.

BURNOUT AND RESILIENCE

In the life cycle of an organization or an individual, there are high points and low points. Challenges give way to successes, plateaus offer momentary resting places, respite turns to complacency, we either reboot or lose our way. Sometimes events threaten to overwhelm us. Both organizations and the individuals who comprise them experience pain. But crisis doesn't last forever; it may actually serve as a catalyst to achieving that next higher plane. Even while the wounds are fresh, the healing begins. Working through the problems that created the crisis is in itself a source of healing.

An African proverb tells us that, "Smooth seas do not make skillful sailors."[12] 12 We all encounter rough seas. For some, over time, that results in burnout. Burnout involves feelings of emotional exhaustion, depersonalization or numbness and a diminished sense of personal accomplishment. The term burnout is often used casually to connote a level of stress, fatigue or frustration, but real burnout is a serious emotional and spiritual state that can affect the individual and the organization.

---

12   Thank you, Neda Kharrazi, Steven White and Sharon Barnes.

Relationship between Workplace Civility and Burnout, 2013 VA All Employee Survey, VA-wide.

All scores significantly (p<.05) different. **Lower burnout scores more favorable.**

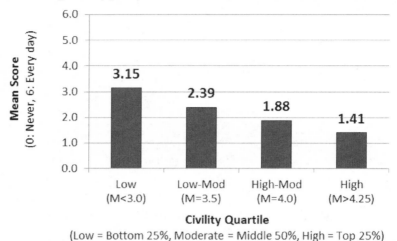

FIGURE 25

In studies done by NCOD, lower burnout was correlated with higher workplace civility[13]13. Some predictors of burnout include the amount and pace of work, working conditions, fairness and recognition, openness to new practices and employee perceptions of whether their organization really cares about them.

In some organizations, first-line supervisors report more burnout, in others, burnout is more prevalent in higher-level managers. There are many possible explanations for this; however, the question prompted NCOD to add a measurement of burnout to the SL 360 to gauge whether Servant Leaders are more or less prone to burnout than traditional leaders. (The jury is still out.)

So why do some people burn out and others bounce back? It's called *resilience*. Resilience is the capacity to bend without breaking. Southwick and Charney (2012) note 10 factors that predispose to resiliency:

---

13   Thank you, Katerine Osatuke.

- Optimism
- Social Support
- Flexibility
- Physical Fitness
- Core Value System
- Faith
- Cognitive Strength
- Facing Fears
- Positive Role Models
- Finding Meaning in Struggles

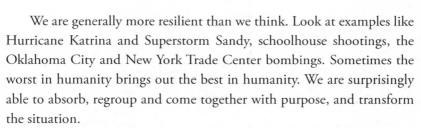

We are generally more resilient than we think. Look at examples like Hurricane Katrina and Superstorm Sandy, schoolhouse shootings, the Oklahoma City and New York Trade Center bombings. Sometimes the worst in humanity brings out the best in humanity. We are surprisingly able to absorb, regroup and come together with purpose, and transform the situation.

Fortunately, the circumstances in which we are called to resilience are rarely of that magnitude, although they may be personally devastating. They largely involve long-term dissatisfaction or disappointment (I can't work here anymore; I've reached the end of my rope); organizational crisis (bankruptcy, loss of public trust, scandal); or individual crisis (loss of a job, loss of a loved one).

We can learn to be resilient in adversity and we start by learning to take care of ourselves.

CARING FOR THE CAREGIVER

This is a phrase used often in health care, where it is well understood that physicians, nurses and other providers are subject to life and death stressors that can deplete them over time. The result? Unhealthy caregivers, burned out caregivers, who are less compassionate and sensitive to the needs of patients, less effective team members, susceptible to error and misjudgment, who withdraw emotionally from their work.

You may not work in health care, but you are undeniably a caregiver. You may be looking after children or aging parents, tending to the less fortunate, providing for a family, protecting the vulnerable. Servant Leaders are caregivers. In the last chapter we discussed the imperative of withdrawal and reflection, of going regularly to the well—whatever your *well* may be—to refresh and replenish.

Taking care of oneself is essential to taking care of others. Holistic interventions like guided imagery, biofeedback, meditation and journaling help some people to relax and refocus. Practices such as reiki, tai chi and yoga are shown to reduce stress, create a greater sense of connectedness, insight and peace.

And here are some other points to consider[14]:

- Try to understand why you are stressed

- Learn your own stress signals

- Reinterpret your stress signals—sometimes what feels like a disaster isn't one

- Avoid stressors when possible

- Take care of your body

- Participate in meaningful, creative work

- Make time for contemplation and appreciation

- Spend time daily with people you enjoy, who lift your spirits

- Volunteer for a cause that inspires you

- You are not indispensable! Learn to let some things go

---

14   Thank you, Dee Ramsel.

> **Adrienne** … who volunteers on behalf of animals, hospice and her
> neighborhood
> **Dee** … for giving people the support and space to find their own
> way
> **Nan** … for her healing presence
> **Leslie** … for her compassion and authenticity
> **Lou Ann** … in her dying she made sure others were at peace
> **Faye** … for practicing true Servant Leadership in the military
> **Gloria** … for her acceptance of people as they are

As Servant Leaders, we have an especially important role in caring for other caregivers. Particularly during times of organizational crisis, leaders can:[15]

- Set an example of self-care: if people see you doing the right things, they will have "permission" to take care of themselves.

- Show support to staff: be sure to address the personal impact of the crisis, show compassion in interactions, assure them that you are there to help, remind staff of their other achievements and your confidence in them.

- Communicate frequently: you may not have all the answers, but share freely and transparently what information you do have, communicate in person, in writing, on video, through newsletters and message boards, and do it repeatedly. Anxious staff may not hear you the first few times.

- Provide safe, convenient opportunities for staff to communicate their concerns. Encourage questions and opinions, engage in walkabouts. Your job is not only to provide facts, but to listen.

Chris and Janet were competing for the same promotion, one that would bring a hefty pay raise. Both were well-qualified, well-liked and tenured. During the protracted interview process, Chris' husband was

---

15   Thank you, Robin Graff-Reed.

injured in an auto accident and consequently lost his job. It appeared he would be unable to get back into the job market for an extended period of time. When Janet learned of this, she consulted with her family and her supervisor, ultimately withdrawing her name from consideration and paving the way for Chris to be offered the post.

This may be one of the most radical stories of selfless service I have ever heard. Some of Janet's co-workers were aghast at her decision and, I'm sorry to say, unsupportive of Chris as a result. But Janet's rationale, clearly stated, was that opportunities to care for each other in life-changing ways don't come along every day. Janet did not see this as a sacrifice, but a gift.

WHY ME? WHAT NEXT?

Servant Leaders faced with such sobering challenges may begin to wonder: "Why me?" I would guess that if you're reading this book, if you are already a student of Servant Leadership, you have earned the respect of colleagues and associates by your education or your experience or your inclination to serve. You have already made an impact on the people you serve, the people with whom you serve and perhaps even on the culture around you.

I'll surmise that you are a systems thinker, seeing connections and relationships wherever you look, and have the ability to see the "big picture." You may be in a position of authority right now, or you may be preparing for one in the future. Whatever your position in life or at work, I imagine you consider seriously how you will translate Servant Leader principles into practice.

Ask:
- What is meaningful to me?
- Why is this important?

> Everybody can be great because anybody can serve. You don't have to have a college degree to serve. You don't have to make your subject and verb agree to serve. You only need a heart full of grace, a soul generated by love.
>
> – Rev. Dr. Martin Luther King, Jr.

- What will I do differently as a Servant Leader?

- What effect will I produce?

- How can being a Servant Leader improve my work? My relationships?

- How can I help my workplace to become a Servant Leader organization?

In a previous chapter we listed next steps for an organization committed to Servant Leadership. But what if your workplace isn't "going there"? Where will you go next—even if your organization won't?

- Talk about Servant Leadership, just increasing awareness raises everybody's game

- Model Servant Leader behaviors and acknowledge them in others

- Have a plan to bring Servant Leadership into your sphere of influence

- Seek to serve in more responsible positions, where you can stimulate change. Your relationships and accomplishments will speak for themselves

- Don't wait for the memo. Use the power you have right now

- Keep practicing…and keep the faith

For years airplane travel has been a regular part of my job. I find it arduous, not only due to the post-9/11 restrictions and inconveniences, but the "mood" that pervades the process. People in airports tend to be tense, angry, rushed and self-absorbed (yes, including myself!) Airport/ airline personnel are often rule-bound, brusque, rushed and defensive. Air travel is less pleasant and less secure than in the past, and all the players sense it.

So in an effort to *see things in a different light*, I created an experiment for myself that I call the Airport Challenge. From the moment I park to arrival at my destination, I search for opportunities to change the collective mood. A smile at the valet, calling the ticket counter clerk by name, a kind word to a TSA officer, acknowledging a wheelchair attendant who has been patient with an irritable customer, a compliment to the flight attendant, switching seats so a family can sit together…you get the idea.

The result of this "experiment"? People sometimes look at me curiously, but they smile back, they call me by name, they thank me—and then they pay it forward. What's more, I feel cheerier, personally connected, patient and forgiving of the small airport slights. I also am more likely to see the better behaviors around me instead of honing in on the worst. I have since expanded to a Mall Challenge and a Post Office Challenge—any place that accumulates and amplifies our flawed human behavior!

REALITY CHECK ✓

Take the Airport Challenge (or the Mall, Post Office, Grocery Store Challenge: choose the place that "pushes your buttons"). "Collect" opportunities to adjust people's attitudes, to soften the irritations. Write them down at the end of your trip and review them. Record your own reactions and the responses of others. Think about any ripple effects that you might have initiated.

All thought creates form on some level. People who reflect deeply inspire results. I think of Dr. S. who contacts his patients in the evening to convey test results or check on how they are feeling. This exceptional practice is a gift of service. Or the colleague who ends every conversation by asking, "What can I do for you today?" Or the leader who, when an employee is not working out, assures *safe passage* to the next job. We are all leaders in service, going the extra mile to help, not because we have to, but because we *can*.

THE LEADER AS FOLLOWER

So which will it be? The truth is, it is not an either/or proposition. We are often simultaneously leaders and followers. No matter how high one sits on the organizational chart, everyone has a boss. If we work for a company, there is always someone to whom we are subordinate, even if it is the Board of Directors or the ultimate consumer. The expectations of a boss, and our relationship to a boss, dramatically frame how we lead.

As a rule, people *lead to please*. I cringe when I recall a time, early in my career, when I said to my boss, "I'm taking care of this problem. I want to make you proud of me." I think now about how my neediness— for my boss to be proud of me—probably shaped the way I approached the problem.

There is certainly nothing wrong with wanting to please the boss, but it is vitally important to recognize the hidden dangers of *leading to please,* of basing our leadership decisions on the anticipated response of one

You might think you're the leader, but you are following something.

– Marianne Williamson

who has hierarchical power over us. Such decisions cannot help but be shaded by self-interest.

Alternatively, Servant Leaders respect each other enough to reward integrity and despise sycophancy. They discern the symbiotic nature of leading and following: that *responsible followership is inherent in the act of leadership.*

We follow in other ways as well. We follow (and are molded by) our personal beliefs, the dictates and doctrines of our organizations and professional disciplines, our chosen career paths, our instincts. We follow the economic, societal and political trends that test our skills of foresight. We follow in a very real sense the needs, expectations, aspirations and ideas of our colleagues, those who report to us, our families and our friends. Servant Leaders take seriously the responsibility of following others in this way, in order to better serve them. Servant Leaders have both the humility and the vision to concede this.

Every leader is delighted by accommodating and engaged followers. But conscientious followership is not blind or unquestioning obedience.

Learning to follow with enthusiasm, perspicacity and moral courage is a virtue. Much as we can be both the child of our parents and the parent of our children, we are concurrently followers and leaders. Understanding what we're following can offer insight into how we are leading, why we are leading and toward what we are leading.

LEGACY

Building a healthy organization, leading to serve in any capacity, is a legacy. Legacy is what we leave behind, a little bit of immortality, an imprint on people's hearts.

Legacy is not about credit. You drop the stone in the water, but can't see how far the ripples spread. The people you touch may never realize it was you who touched them: they just experience your *effect*. Success is great, but significance is even better.

A legacy is an endowment: one that has been constructed piece by piece, has been tried and tested, nurtured and strengthened, has persevered in its value and its timelessness. A legacy is not dropped like a bolt from the blue at the culmination of a career; it is accumulated day by day, year by year, action by action. *We are known by the legacies we create long before we leave them.*

You are conceiving your legacy right now. Begin today to think about it, see it forming around you. Be deliberate in its design. You are building a monument: your acts and relationships are the bricks, your thoughts and intentions the mortar. **We are all leaders, all the time.**

A culture of service cannot happen without *you*. In a world where all things are connected, *you* spark the charge,

you bridge the synapse,

you ignite the arc,

you complete the circuit.

All Things Connected...

 Several years ago I took part in a program where we were encouraged to write our own *Legacy Statements*. These statements were intensely personal, a kind of introspective GPS reading, and meant to be private. But throughout this book I've shared many of my deepest thoughts. I see no reason to stop now...

For many years I've carried an unspoken conviction,
   A persistent refrain,
   An unrelenting thread
Moving quietly through the tasks and challenges of my leadership:
   A belief in the genuine power of service,
      The untapped potential of each worker,
      The razor-thin margin dividing accountability and trust,
      The primacy of collaboration over competition,
        The linkage of engaged staff, esteemed customer and organizational excellence.
This is for me the fine line between drowning and walking on water.

But on occasion
The stars align,
Intentions converge,
And the time is clearly right to give voice to those ideas.

In an edgy, evolving environment of metrics and technology,
   Hierarchy and politics,
My organization has given me that voice, nurtured that passion,
Allowed the space to shape a culture-centered approach—

Part philosophy,
    Part physics,
    Part pragmatism,
To the business of health care.

For me, this work has reinforced certain truths:
    That the carrot is mightier than the stick;
    That people who are beaten into submission carry wounds;
    That the inherent chaos of our jobs must be securely bracketed
        Between an unambiguous mission
        And an uncompromising corporate character;
    That the "soft skills" are really the "hard skills;"
    That justice and respect drive out fear,
        And that, where fear resides, growth is not possible;
        That there is wisdom in living and modeling a balanced life,
        In being able to say "no" while delighting in saying "yes!"
            That what we do is truly important, but how we do it is
            even more so.

I would like to think that I've helped to raise this awareness,
Stimulate this discourse,
By weaving it into the fabric of my leadership.
I've been permitted to create, cultivate and perseverate on the notion
    That all things are connected,
    That we're all made of the same cosmic "stuff,"
        That while we dance to the tunes of metrics, mandates and
        bottom lines,
        What we'll ultimately be judged on is the quality and com-
        passion of our relationships.

We are only as good as the people we lead:
If we're singing solo, we've lost the chorus.

Some call that Servant Leadership.
Some call it Tao.

I call it common sense.
In human organizations, the means justify the ends.

My legacy is neither flashy nor splashy;
Not a tangible accomplishment,
Enterprising project
Or cutting edge development.
My legacy is passed on to those who resonate with it,
And those who don't yet know that they do.

I leave a theme,
A thread,
A slow, soft, steady drumbeat.

...All Things Connected

TOOLBOX ACTIVITY:
Servant Leader Interviews

Select a partner who, like you, is on a journey of Servant Leadership. Find a quiet spot where you won't be interrupted and interview your partner using the questions below. Then turn the tables and let that person interview you. This should take about 30 minutes.

1. For you, what is the relationship between service and leadership?

2. How do you demonstrate Servant Leadership now?

3. How are you being called to lead (and perhaps turning a deaf ear)?

4. What role does courage play in Servant Leadership?

5. Do you ever struggle with being a good Servant Leader and a good work/community leader? How does that feel? How do you reconcile the two?

6. What barriers exist to practicing Servant Leadership?

7. How do you maintain integrity as a Servant Leader when things around you are changing?

8. Given that you are not a Servant Leader until others see you as one, what characteristics and behaviors do you want to define your identity?

9. Do you think Servant Leadership is countercultural? Why?

10. How can you create more Servant Leaders at work?

❧ Discussion ❧

With your partner, think about the following:

- Which questions were the most difficult to answer? The easiest?

- Were you more comfortable with the theoretical questions or the practical ones?

- Were any of your partner's responses surprising?

- Did thinking through your Servant Leadership in this depth help you consider next steps in your development?

- Did your partner offer any useful insights?

- Did listening to another's experience in Servant Leadership give you a sense of support?

- Support is important as we struggle to be Servant Leaders. How could you build a support system?

TOOLBOX ACTIVITY:
Legacy: Creating a Testimonial

❧ Instructions ☙

You are selected to receive a lifetime achievement award from a prestigious national association. The Program Committee has asked you to draft your own testimonial, which will be presented at the award ceremony. Engage in some thoughtful self-examination as you write a narrative. Include details about your accomplishments, goals, regrets, values, why you believe you won this award, how you would like to be remembered and anything else that will paint a picture of who you are for this audience. Note: your parents, spouse, children, boss and best friend will be in attendance. When you are finished, ask a trusted friend or colleague to read the testimonial out loud to you.

_____

_____

_____

_____

_____

_____

_____

_____

_____

_____

✿ Discussion ✿

- What was this exercise like for you?

- What was the easiest part? The hardest part?

- What was the impact of knowing your family would be there?

- Was there a difference in writing your testimonial and hearing it read aloud?

- Did this exercise help you to see yourself more clearly? To appreciate yourself more honestly?

- Did it suggest any changes in your life?

❧ Chapter References ❦

Frick, D. (2004). Robert K. Greenleaf: A Life of Servant Leadership. San Francisco, CA: Berrett-Koehler.

Greenleaf, R. K. (2002) Servant Leadership: A Journey into the Nature of Legitimate Power and Greatness. New York: Paulist Press.

Henley, D. and Frey, G. (1973). Desperado. Cass County Music/Red Cloud Music.

Keith, K. (2012). Questions and Answers about Servant Leadership. Westfield, IN: The Greenleaf Center for Servant Leadership.

Lanza, R. and Berman, B. (2009). 'Biocentrism': How life creates the universe. www.nbcnews.com

Southwick, S. and Charney, D. (2012). Resilience: The Science of Mastering Life's Greatest Challenges. Cambridge, UK: Cambridge University Press.

Williamson, M. (2016). https://livestream.com

APPENDIX

REFERENCES AND BIBLIOGRAPHY

Belton, L. (Fall 2013) Organizational Health Newsletter Vol. 20.

Biron, C., Burke, R. J. and Cooper, C. L. (2014). Creating Healthy Workplaces. Surrey, England: Gower Publishing.

Bruhn, J. (2001). Trust and the Health of Organizations. New York: Kluwer Academic/Plenum Publishers.

Cameron, K. S. and Quinn, R. E. (2011). Diagnosing and Changing Organizational Culture. San Francisco, CA: Jossey-Bass.

Capra, F. (1991). The Tao of Physics. Boston, MA: Shambala Press.

Cerit, Y. (2009). The effects of Servant Leader behaviors of school principals on teachers' job satisfaction. Educational Management Administration and Leadership, 37 (5), 600-623.

Chand, S. (2015). William Ouchi's Theory Z of Motivation. www.articlelibrary. com/motivation/william-ouchis-theory-z-of-motivation

Chinese Physicists Measure Speed of "Spooky Action at a Distance." MIT Technology Review, March 7, 2013.

Chittister, J. (2004). Called to Question: A Spiritual Memoir. Lanham, MD: Sheed and Ward.

Church, D. (2005). Einstein's Business: Engaging Soul, Imagination and Excellence in the Workplace. Santa Rosa, CA: www.EliteBooksOnline.com

Collins, J. (2001). Good to Great. New York: Harper Business.

Comte-Sponville, A. (2002). A Small Treatise on the Great Virtues. New York: Henry Holt.

Deming, W. E., (1982). Out of the Crisis. Cambridge, MA: The MIT Press.

Drucker, P. (1954). The Practice of Management. New York: Harper Business.

Dutton, J. E. (2003). Energize Your Workplace: How to Create and Sustain High-Quality Connections at Work. San Francisco, CA: Jossey-Bass.

Erhart, M. G. (2004). Leadership and Procedural Justice Climate as Antecedents of Unit Level Organizational Citizenship Behaviors. Personnel Psychology, 57, 61-94.

Farling, M. L., Stone, A. G. and Winston, B. E. (1999). Servant Leadership: Setting the Stage for Empirical Research. Journal of Leadership Studies, 6, 49-62.

Foundation for Inner Peace. (1996). A Course in Miracles. New York: Viking Penguin.

Frick, D. (2004). Robert K. Greenleaf: A Life of Servant Leadership. San Francisco, CA: Berrett-Koehler.

Frick, D. (2013). Lessons You Can Use from the Life of Robert K. Greenleaf. Presented at the International Conference on Servant Leadership, Indianapolis, IN.

Greenleaf, R. K. (1970). The Servant as Leader. Atlanta, GA. The Greenleaf Center for Servant Leadership.

Greenleaf, R. K. (2009). The Institution as Servant. Westfield, IN: The Greenleaf Center for Servant Leadership.

Greenleaf, R. K. (2013). Servant: Retrospect and Prospect. Westfield, IN: Greenleaf Center for Servant Leadership.

Greenleaf, R. K. (2002) Servant Leadership: A Journey into the Nature of Legitimate Power and Greatness. New York: Paulist Press.

Hawkins, D. R. (1995). Power vs Force. USA: Hay House.

Henley, D. and Frey, G. (1973). Desperado. Cass County Music/Red Cloud Music.

Hersey, P. and Blanchard, K. H. (1969). Life Cycle Theory of Leadership. Training and Development Journal, Vol. 23 (5), 26-34.

Holmes, J. A., www.quotationspage.com

House, R. J. (Sep. 1971). A Path Goal Theory of Leadership Effectiveness. Administrative Science Quarterly, Vol. 16, No 3, 321-339.

Hu, J. and Liden, R. C. (2011). Antecedents of team potency and team effectiveness: An examination of goal and process clarity and servant leadership. Journal of Applied Psychology, 1-12.

Irving, J. A. and Longbotham, G. J. (2007). Team effectiveness and six essential themes: a Regression model based on items in the organizational leadership assessment. International Journal of Leadership Studies, 2 (2), 98-113.

Jaramillo, F., Grisaffe, D. B., Chonko, L. B. and Roberts, J. A. (2009b). Examining the impact of Servant Leadership on salesperson's turnover intention. Journal of Personal Selling and Sales Management, 29 (4), 351-365.

Jennings, K. and Stahl-Wert, J. (2004). The Serving Leader. San Francisco, CA: Berrett-Koehler.

Jung, C. (1959). The Archetypes and the Collective Unconscious. Princeton, NJ: Princeton University Press.

Keith, K. M. (2008.) The Case for Servant Leadership. Westfield IN: Greenleaf Center for Servant Leadership.

Keith, K. M. (2012). Questions and Answers about Servant Leadership. Westfield, IN: The Greenleaf Center for Servant Leadership.

Keith, K. M. (2013). Growing to Greatness through Servant Leadership. www.toservefirst.com/...Growing to Greatness%20through-Servant-Leadership

Keith, K. M. (2013). The Ethical Advantage of Servant Leadership. Singapore: The Greenleaf Centre for Servant Leadership (Asia).

Keith, K. M. (2015). The Christian Leader at Work. Honolulu, HI: Terrace Press.

Kesey, K. (1963). One Flew Over the Cuckoo's Nest. New York: Signet.

Lanza, R. and Berman, B. (2009). 'Biocentrism': How life creates the universe. www.nbcnews.com

Lao Tzu. Tao Te Ching. Verse 17. Acc6.its.brooklyn.cuny.edu/~phalsall/texts/taote

LeaderServe Workshop. (2005). Magellan Executive Resources, Minneapolis, MN.

Laub, J.A. (1999). Assessing the servant organization: Development of the servant organization leadership assessment instrument. Dissertation Abstracts International, 60, (02), 308.

Lipton, B. (2007). The Biology of Belief. New York: Hay House.

Longman, P. (2012). The Best Care Anywhere. San Francisco, CA: Berrett-Koehler Publishers.

MacGregor, D. (1960). The Human Side of Enterprise. New York: McGraw-Hill.

Mead, M. www.brainyquotes.com

McCarren, H., Lewis-Smith, J., Belton, L., Yanovsky, B., Robinson, J. and Osatuke, K. (2016) Creation of a Multi-Rater Feedback Assessment for the Development of Servant Leaders in the Veterans Health Administration. Servant Leadership: Theory and Practice, Vol. 3, (1), 12-51.

McCluhan, M., www.brainyquote.com

Merton, T. (1966). Conjectures of a Guilty Bystander. New York: Doubleday.

Northouse, P. G. (1997). Leadership: Theory and Practice. USA: Sage Publications.

Nouwen, H. (1975). Reaching Out. New York: Doubleday.

Oshry, Barry www.powerandsystems.com. Organization Workshop.

Parris, D. L. and Peachey, J. W. (2013). A systemic literature review of Servant Leadership Theory in Organizational Contexts. Journal of Business Ethics, 113, 377-393.

Patrnchak, J. M. (2016). The Engaged Enterprise. Atlanta, GA: Greenleaf Center for Servant Leadership.

Patterson, K. (2003). Servant Leadership: A Theoretical Model. Dissertation Abstracts, International, 64 (2), 570.

Perry, S. (2008). Society for Neuroscience, Nov. 16.

Shakespeare, W. (1596). The Merchant of Venice. Act IV, Scene 1. www.poets.org

Sheldrake, R. (March 2016) www.sheldrake.org. Morphic Resonance and Morphic Fields.

Shinsecki, Gen. E., (2001). www.brainyquotes.com

Sipe, J. W. and Frick, D. M. (2009, 2015). Seven Pillars of Servant Leadership. New York/New Jersey: Paulist Press.

Spears, L. (1998). Insights into Leadership: Service, Stewardship, Spirit and Servant Leadership. New York: Wiley.

Spears, L. (2005). On Character and Servant Leadership: Ten characteristics of effective, caring leaders. Westfield, IN: Greenleaf Center for Servant Leadership.

Southwick, S. and Charney, D. (2012). Resilience: The Science of Mastering Life's Greatest Challenges, Cambridge, UK: Cambridge University Press.

Walumbwa, F. O. (2010). Servant leadership, procedural justice climate, service climate and organizational citizenship behavior: a Cross-level investigation. Journal of Applied Psychology, 95, (3), 517-529.

Wheatley, M. (2006). Leadership and the New Science. San Francisco, CA: Berrett-Koehler Publishers.

Williamson, M. (2016). https://livestream.com

Williamson, M. www.inspiringquotes.us

Williamson, M. www.AZQuotes.com

Wong, P. T. P. and Davey, D. (2007). Best Practices in Servant Leadership. Paper presented at the Servant Leadership Research Roundtable, Regent University, Virginia Beach, VA.

www.usccb.org/bible/matthew/10

INDEX OF FIGURES

AFTERWORD

After hanging on the words of the Servant Leader gurus for years, I could not imagine having anything to say, at least anything worth saying. I was doubtful that I could add any new value to the Servant Leader conversation. Whether I accomplished that or not is up to the reader.

The process of writing, the discipline of sifting through the thoughts and learning of 40 years, was a mountaintop experience: at once enlightening, humbling, joyful and therapeutic. If there are errors or oversights within, please pardon them. My tendency is to view conventional wisdom from a slightly unconventional perspective.

I am hopeful that something in this book helps the reader take another step, turn another corner and feel "companioned" on the journey.

ACKNOWLEDGEMENTS

With heartfelt thanks...

To my VA NCOD colleagues, who have made the cause of Servant Leadership their own...

To my Servant Leader guides and gurus, and to the Greenleaf Center for Servant Leadership and its Board of Trustees, past and present...

To the shining stars of Servant Leadership in my life, some of whom were mentioned in this book and many who were not. Your names are all written in my heart...

ABOUT LINDA W. BELTON

Linda W. Belton served as a Senior Executive in the Veterans Health Administration for 20 years, from 1995 to 2008, as Director, Veterans Integrated Service Network, leading a region of VA hospitals and clinics in the Midwest, and from 2008 until 2015, as VA's first Director of Organizational Health and as Deputy Director, National Center for Organization Development.

In these roles she has spoken to national and international audiences on topics of Organizational Health, including civility and Servant Leadership. As part of an enthusiastic team, she created the CREW initiative (Civility, Respect and Engagement in the Workplace), which has been widely used in VA, endorsed by the Joint Commission and replicated internationally. She introduced and organized programs in Servant Leadership within the Veterans Health Administration, building the foundation for VHA's intensive and ongoing efforts.

Prior to her work in VA, Linda was appointed by the Governor of Wisconsin to lead the State Hospital system, a post she held for nine years, and served in executive leadership positions at a variety of private sector health care organizations.

Linda holds an RN from Jameson Memorial Hospital School of Nursing in New Castle, Pennsylvania, a BS from the University of the State of New York, and an MS from Columbia Pacific University. She was a Johnson Fellow at the Harvard University JFK School of Government's program for Senior Executives in State and Local Government, completed the VA Executive Fellows program and the University of Rochester's program in Leading Organizations to Health.

During her career, she received honors including: three Presidential Rank Awards (Meritorious and Distinguished Executive), the Distinguished Service Award (American Society of Public Administration) and the Women in Government Award. Linda is a Lifetime Fellow in the American College of Healthcare Executives (LFACHE). She served on the Board of Trustees of the Greenleaf Center for Servant Leadership (2011-2015), is a certified Nurse Executive (American Nursing Association) and a certified Mentor Fellow. Linda has been a lay Associate of the Sisters of the Sorrowful Mother since 1985.

Linda has co-authored the following publications:

McCarren, H., Lewis-Smith, J., Belton, L., Yanovsky, B., Robinson, J., and Osatuke, K. (2016). Creation of a Multi-Rater Feedback Assessment for the Development of Servant Leaders in the Veterans Health Administration. Servant Leadership: Theory and Practice, Vol. 3, (1), 12-51.

Belton, L. (2008-2015). VA Organizational Health Newsletter.

Osatuke K., Cash, M., Belton, L., and Dyrenforth , S. R. (2014). Civility, Respect, and Engagement in the Workplace (CREW): Creating organizational environments that work for all. In C. Biron, R. Burke, and C. Cooper (Eds.) Creating healthy workplaces: Stress reduction, improved well-being, and organizational effectiveness. London: Gower Publishing.

Osatuke, K., Draime, J., Moore, S., Ramsel, D., Meyer, A., Barnes, S., Belton, L, Dyrenforth, S. (2012). Organization Development in the Department of Veterans Affairs. T Miller (Ed) The Praeger Handbook of Veterans' Health. Santa Barbara: ABC-CLIO, LLC.

Osatuke, K., Moore, S. C., Ward, C., Dyrenforth, S. R., and Belton, L. (2009). Civility, Respect, Engagement in the Workforce (CREW): Nationwide organization development intervention at Veterans Health Administration. The Journal of Applied Behavioral Science, 45(3), 384-410.

Belton, L., Dyrenforth, S. (2007). Civility in the Workplace. Healthcare Executive.

Belton, L., Hodgson, M. (2004). Violence in Healthcare Facilities: Lessons Learned from the Veterans Health Administration. American College of Occupational and Environmental Medicine.

Linda currently lives with her husband in Ann Arbor, Michigan, and has two adult children. She is an avid reader, musician, and poet.

Proof

Made in the USA
Charleston, SC
18 November 2016